THE SCHOOL THAT CARED

A Story of the Marva Collins Preparatory School of Cincinnati

P. Kamara Sekou Collins

University Press of America,® Inc.
Dallas · Lanham · Boulder · New York · Oxford

⊖∞™ The paper used in this publication meets the minimum
requirements of American National Standard for Information
Sciences—Permanence of Paper for Printed Library Materials,
ANSI Z39.48—1984

I dedicate this book to all of those people who have strived to provide a better way for children through The Marva Collins Preparatory School of Cincinnati. Your stories deserve to grace the pages of many more books.

Contents

Preface

In the fall of 1995, I departed Florida A&M University as a fledgling teacher to complete my student-teaching internship at The Marva Collins Preparatory School in Cincinnati Ohio (MCPSC). I can vividly remember my initial perceptions of this school community. I had visited Cincinnati with a college baseball teammate (his hometown) during a college break a year or so prior to the internship with no idea that MCPSC even existed. Like many college students, upon his arrival from our university in Florida it was customary that he go to visit all of his closest relatives to receive hugs, kisses, and inform them of his collegiate progress. I joined him on these visits, one of which took us to his godmother's house to assemble a bicycle for his god-brother's birthday. This was the life-changing day in which I became aware of The Marva Collins Preparatory School of Cincinnati.

I had both read and heard quite a bit about the Marva Collins Way through course work at Florida A&M University, a HBCU (Historically Black Colleges and Universities). In my school's Education Department, Mrs. Collins was an icon, but I had never had the chance to meet her or any student who attended her schools. At the time, I did not know of a Marva Collins School in Ohio, as the well-known Westside Preparatory School created by Mrs. Collins was located in Illinois. Nevertheless, as my teammate and I tightened screws on his god-brother's new bicycle, I was impressed with the 7-year-old African-American boy's ability to articulate his perspectives on various issues. He was not shy or arrogant, just confident. He was knowledgeable enough about world events to the point of following our conversation, which I thought unusual for a second grader. This led me to ask my teammate, "you all must have some pretty good public schools around here." He responded, "nah, he goes to The Marva Collins School." This response was surprising bearing in mind the fact that I only knew of Mrs. Collins' school in Chicago.

This entire affair ended with me inquiring about further information from the young boy's mother on how to get in contact with this school. When I returned to Florida, I began to explore the possibility of a student-teaching experience at MCPSC. A student-teaching placement worked out nicely, and I secured lodging for a semester in a hotel a few miles from the school, at the school's President/CEO, Dr. Mims' expense. My time spent at The Marva Collins Preparatory School of Cincinnati introduced me to some of the hardest working and caring teachers that I have ever known. Others must read and know of such worthy educators. And, as fate would have it, approximately five years later, I returned and spent over a year working and conducting research with this school. An ethic of care seems to permeate from this school community in a way that is unique and worth capturing in some form as to allow future generations to continue such a worthy tradition.

Part I

Reflecting on our History

Chapter 1

Cincinnati, Blacks, and Education in the 19th Century

On a warm, summer's evening in the heart of downtown, I sit at Fountain Square listening to "1230 The Buzz" on my small radio and absorb a taste of what *Places Rated Almanac* has rated as one of the most livable cities in the United States. Just a few blocks to the south of downtown "Cinci" flows the Ohio River that attracted many early Europeans to the area. Historically, for many enslaved Africans crossing the Ohio River symbolically meant the difference between "being free and being enslaved."

The heart of downtown "Cinci" presents a myriad of what seems to be city locals shopping, coming from work, or heading to one of the downtown taverns for an evening relaxer. Also, tourists with cameras around their necks capture my attention as they look up at superstructures like the Carew Tower, Cincinnati's largest building, which as legend has it was built in less than a year during the Great Depression as countless eager workers chipped in on the labor. People of all kinds seem to fill the streets on this Saturday evening. From all directions I can see the young and old, familiar ethnic looking individuals and others of whom I have no clue, the corporate America business types and the casual dresser-downers, the baggy hip-hop kinds (not only African-Americans either), and those of the elderly golden years. People are all over the place! I just sit and watch as people go about their business; the leisurely horse carriage slowly strolls by as I watch the sunset behind the city's symbol, the Tyler Davidson Fountain—wondering who on earth was Tyler Davidson? For that matter, who was Carew of Carew Tower?

Randall Robinson's work, *The Debt,* a groundbreaking treatment of African-Americans and reparations, highlights how the symbols and larger than life statues at the Mall in the nation's capital seem to make for an interesting kind of European-American ancestral worship. It is a type of ancestral worshipping ritual that was created and is preserved with every segment of multiethnic U.S. America's tax dollars. I wonder if I am witnessing the same thing on Fountain Square as I look at the sculptures here and there, or the quite foreign names on the buildings. Is this myriad of local taxpayers going by in every direction on this nice summer's evening suffering the same plight through their state and federal tax contributions? Let us not even mention the Ohio city taxes which take Mr. Robinson's constant reiterations of *"They have taken* my *tax dollars and bought only what* they *need,"* to another level (pp. 54-56).

As I am observing the diversity around Fountain Square and wondering about the lack of equity in the distribution of tax dollars, my mind drifts to the state of affairs in the city's educational system. I begin to wonder about the failure of the State legislature to twice meet the Ohio Supreme Courts ruling for an equal and fair system of funding for the state's public schools over the past several years. While, during the same period of time, the general assembly passed two bills that were signed into law by the Governor further raising academic standards and accountability in the inequitably funded schools. The radio announces that the most recent police killing of an African-American male is the fifteenth African-American male killed by the Cincinnati police in the past 5 years. One of the "most livable cities in America" is about to explode in anger.

Historicizing African-Americans and Education in Cincinnati

Following the American Revolutionary War, four primary European groups began to make claims against the indigenous natives for the lands immediately north of the Ohio river: the New Englanders to the northeast, the Pennsylvanians in the central section of the state, and Virginians and Kentuckians to the south. Other foreign born immigrants entered the area coming from Germany and Ireland. After going through several name changes such as Ft. Washington and Losantville, the area was finally declared Cincinnati by General Arthur St. Clair, then governor of the Northwest Territory, in 1802. Carter G. Woodson (1875-1950) brings light to this same period's post American Revolutionary War temperament of those of European descent towards Africans around the Northwest Territory. Woodson states,

> As the reaction following the era of good feeling toward the Negroes during the Revolutionary period had not reached its climax, free persons of color had been content to remain in the South. The unexpected immigration of these Negroes into this section and the last bold effort made to drive them out marked epochs in their history in this city. The history of these people prior to the Civil War, therefore, falls into three periods, one of toleration from 1800 to 1826, one of persecution from 1826 to 1841, and one of amelioration from 1841 to 1861. (excerpt in Dabney, 1926, p. 31)

Born the son of ex-enslaved Africans, Woodson was able to enter high school at the age of twenty moving on from W. Virginia to Berea College in Kentucky for undergraduate training. Woodson went on to become the second person of African descent, after W.E.B Dubois, to receive a Ph.D. in history. As a Harvard graduate and founder of National Negro History Week (now black History month), Woodson studied the lives of African people in Cincinnati. Although it had been noted that there were no Negroes in Hamilton County before 1800, Woodson could not determine exactly how many persons of color were in the area during the opening decade of the 1800s. Yet, his research did reveal that a real exodus of free Negroes and fugitives from the South did not begin prior to 1815 (Dabney, 1926). Based on Woodson's account, we can make inferences in respect of the earliest possible inception of Cincinnati's role in the enslaved African freeing institution, "the underground railroad."

Along with Woodson's general assessment of this epoch's human temperament, Macke (1999) becomes quite instrumental in further problematizing his three general historical periods. For, as Woodson explored the general European/white temperament towards Africans, Macke delved into the groups' differing geo-cultural backgrounds stating,

> New Englanders tended to be tolerant of Negro migration; many Quakers from Pennsylvania, as well as some of the southern states, opposed slavery and tolerated the presence of people of color; and southerners from Virginia and Kentucky were, for the most part, quite hostile and

> anti-Negro because many were small farmers who had left the south to
> avoid the competition of slave labor. German and Irish workers also
> feared competition from Negro labor. (Macke, 1999, p. 4)

Taken as a whole, the combination of Woodson (1916) and Macke's
(1999) snapshots of post-Revolutionary – pre-Civil war Cincinnati becomes even clearer when contextualized with the newly forming legislative policies of the day. The question of, "What shall we do with the
Negroes" came up in the Northwest Territory's Constitutional Conven-
tion of 1802. Woodson's research revealed that the Negroes along with
the Indigenous Native Americans and foreigners were simply left out of
the newly organized political structure due to the word "WHITE" en-
shrined in the law, which was a clever measure to maintain the domi-
nance and power of people classified as white. Hence, those people classified as white would be subject to all of the rights and privileges of the
newly conquered territory even though there was no scientific way to
determine who was and was not white. Moreover, a law was enacted
providing that no Negro or mulatto should be able to remain permanently
in the newly forming state, unless he/she could present a court issued
certificate of freedom (Dabney, 1926).

Now, pointing the new policy "finger" at sympathetic whites of the
region, the legislation went on to codify that a Negro was unemployable
without a certificate of freedom. Any white person that risked hiring,
harboring, or hindering the capture of an African person without a certificate of freedom could be fined $50. Several years later, the $50 dollars fine was increased to $100 as to provide the informer compensation
for "snitching" as well. In addition, if these laws were not absurd enough,
in 1807 the legislature enacted another measure that made life more un-
bearable for Africans. New legislation now required no African person
to settle in Ohio unless he/she could pay a $500 bond to *supposedly*
ensure his or her good behavior and city support (Dabney, 1926). With
the above stated legal imperatives in mind, the new "free state" legislature also provided white protection from Negro evidence while simultaneously depriving persons of color of jury duty privileges. Finally, these
provisions, which came to be known as "The Black Laws," made it
policy to prohibit the education of Negroes at public expense in 1829.

Even with the unjust "Black Laws" of the land, African people per-
sisted in providing forms of education for themselves. Historian John B.
Shotwell found that Henry Collins initiated the first school for African

people in an old pork house (some say carpenter shop). With a colored population of approximately 250, Cincinnati's first school of this kind lasted less than a year (Dabney, 1926). Also, in exploring the early to mid-nineteenth century several African-operated private schools briefly appeared then disappeared with ill equipped teachers but a strong desire for some form of education. Alluding to such a strong desire for knowledge Macke shares,

> It was not until 1834 that the first successful Negro elementary school was established by Owen T. B. Nickens, from Virginia. One historian later noted that "tuition was $1, none turned away for lack of payment." Nickens taught in this school until 1849. . . . (1999, p. 11)

Pushed to the margins of the city in shanty wooden tenements, the people of what came to be known as Bucktown and Little Africa continued to struggle in the "free" north.

The "let's help them go back to Africa" sentiment was also present in white Cincinnati during the early to mid-nineteenth century, and many blacks seemed to have seriously considered such an idea. A tract of land containing 10,000 acres, lying north of Liberia, between that republic and Sierra Leone was purchased by some white Cincinnatians for this purpose. This newly purchased area was called "Ohio in Africa" and blacks were urged to go there and settle (Dabney, 1926). One might find the historical account of this "Back to Africa" attempt rather intriguing.

Baker Jones, a gentleman of African descent from Mercer County was summoned to lead such a colony. Jones considered this offer by the proposing white Cincinnatians but declined after not receiving all that he demanded in preparation for such an endeavor. Peter H. Clark (who later became a prominent African leader, educator and principal) did accept to lead this voyage of one hundred and nineteen passengers but had a change of heart after reaching New Orleans and refusing to embark on the dirty schooner chartered for the trip. Others decided to continue without Clark and those not willing to complete the voyage due to lack of trust in this vessel.

Unfortunately, those voyagers who decided to continue their trip back to Africa were struck by smallpox shortly after their departure. The lumber schooner's captain finally docked in Charleston, S.C. for medical attention. Those considered uninfected by the smallpox breakout were held in a jail for entering Charleston in contravention of state law. The story ends solemnly as it is documented that after lingering in South Carolina for approximately three months, the survivors were freed and set out again on their journey. Most of the passengers died rendering the emigration attempt a failure (Dabney, 1926).

Some white abolitionist leaders and philanthropists did provide invaluable assistance to the growing Negro population of Cincinnati leading to the middle of the nineteenth century. Yet, there remained a continued need for struggle in the arena of educational policy from the state down to the local level. This assistance helped create a new level of leadership amongst the black community of Cincinnati. Within the social and legal context of both the city and state, black leaders struggled to gain access to educational opportunities for their youth. Much to their credit, the black leaders and other sympathizers convinced Ohio legislators to vote in favor of allowing public support for colored children by 1849 (Macke, 1999). The Africans of Cincinnati and their leaders continuously fought within the limits of such unjust human constructed laws for access to the educational arena, even with seemingly insurmountable odds. Blacks were being regarded as intruders by white citizens, denounced as idle and criminal, kept out of hotels, theaters, and all public places frequented by white residents.

During the same period, the Presbyterian influenced Lane Seminary was founded in 1832. Lane Seminary "got the ball rolling" towards progressive ends as students of this school formed the Anti-Slavery Society. Directed by Lyman Beecher, father of Harriet Beecher Stowe, there began to be much debate over unjust slave ideology. Nevertheless, the strong anti-African dissent of the day squelched those tendencies, thus forcing many sympathizers to transfer to Oberlin institute on the condition that the school would admit Negroes.

The primary instruction of Augustus Wattles and the help of four women from New York responding to a newspaper advertisement spearheaded the former Lane Seminary students. The group began to provide tutelage in various subjects including religion, grammar, and natural philosophy to hundreds of Africans in Cincinnati. African students excelled in this new educational setting according their teachers a high level of respect. The environment was observed to be in good order and attention to study was central. Moreover, observers reported that the school seemed to have a feeling of connectedness between the students and the teachers (Macke, 1999).

Thus, throughout the first half of the nineteenth century, the dim light of finding themselves in Cincinnati between "rocks and hard places" former enslaved Africans began to improve educationally as well as economically. We can begin to construct an even clearer mental picture of Cincinnati during what Carter G. Woodson labeled, "the periods of persecution (1826 to 1841) and amelioration (1841 to 1861)." For, during both periods, persecution and amelioration occurred simultaneously—depending on the group of European/whites in question.

Thus, with the help of the liberal minded white segment of the city, a new leadership emerged amongst the African community. This era clearly displays an understanding by the blacks for the need of some type of formal education by 1835. According to Woodson (1916), "Prior to this period they had been unable to make any sacrifices for charity and education. . . In 1839, however, the colored people raised $889.30 for this purpose" (excerpt in Dabney, p. 38). In addition, Cleveland played host to the state's first Convention of Colored Men. This group organized the School Fund Society, and within a few years, they had built schoolhouses in Cincinnati, Columbus, Springfield, and Cleveland (Macke, 1999). Unfortunately, within two years Cincinnati members had disengaged themselves while still maintaining political links as the group fought to repeal the unjust Black Laws of the land.

Within a year of the $889.30 school finance campaign, Woodson's research further alludes to the African desire for some form of education. By 1840, two schools led by Reverend Denham and Mr. Goodwin had sixty-five pupils with students paying $3 per quarter. Another school headed by Miss Merrill had forty-seven pupils paying the same $3 fee (Dabney, 1926). Woodson goes on to state, "It was in fact a brighter day for the colored people. In 1840 an observer said that they had improved faster than any other people in the city" (p. 39).

Springing from the new upswing in momentum, Africans were assisted once more by a son of an area banker and Yale graduate anti-slave proponent, Rev. Hiram Gilmore. For a brief five years (1844-1849), the creation of the African attended Cincinnati High School under the guidance of Rev. Gilmore produced some of the more notable African leaders of the day such as: P.B.S. Pinchback, John M. Langston, Thomas Ball, and Monroe Trotter. P.B.S. Pinchback rose to become Lieutenant Governor of Louisiana. John M. Langston became a Virginia Congressman, Dean of Howard University's Law School, as well as Minister to Haiti. Thomas Ball became a well-respected artist, and Monroe Trotter became the United States Recorder of Deeds under President Cleveland. In addition, two graduates, Peter Clark and John I. Gaines, both went on to graduate from Oberlin College and lead the battle for educating black children in Cincinnati (Macke, 1999).

Much of the success as well as failures of Africans in the city of Cincinnati leading the mid-nineteenth century had occurred outside of the School Tax Fund Law of 1829, which was designed for white public schooling but surely not for the benefit of Africans. Moreover, most whites of the epoch wanted their schools "pure!" There were black property owners at this time that paid taxes as well as the scam-like $500 dollars "good faith and support" bond money just to settle in Cincinnati within 60 days of their arrival (the original time frame was 20 days but the blacks appealed for 90 and was given 60 by city officials). Yet, the white supremacist ideology and institutional force of the day created the illusion in most whites' minds that it was "moral" and "decent" to not allow Africans to benefit from public education, even if they were taxpayers. These whites wanted their schools "pure" to the point of having mulatto purges, ala witch hunts, to make sure that only "pure whites" got the benefit of public funded schooling.

One example of such white supremacist feelings occurred in a schoolhouse in 1849. Several belligerent parents complained that children of color were being allowed to attend school with their "pure" white children. Actually, the plaintiffs were correct, there were two children whose father was white and their mother mulatto in attendance at the school. To address the complaint, the school principal asked the complaining parents to point out the undesirable pupils attending the school. This turned out to be an impossible task for the complaining parents as the mulatto students were less dark than many of the white pupils in the school and two of the school's best students (Dabney, 1926).

Nevertheless, although other "Black Laws" remained intact, by 1849 at least the educational aspect of these unjust laws had been successfully repealed; and a split between the Whigs and the Democrats in the Ohio General Assembly yielded favorable legislation for the Africans. Woodson (1916) states, "Abolitionists, Free Soilers and Whigs fearlessly attacked the laws which kept the Negroes under legal and economic disabilities" (Dabney, p. 43). According to Macke, the legislation mandated,

> School districts to establish separate common schools for black children if there were twenty or more black children in the district and if

the district officials felt it inadvisable to admit the Negro children to the existing schools serving white children. The law required school districts to compile tax lists for Negro residents and to take a census of Negro children. Taxes collected from black taxpayers would be used for the support of schools for their children. (p. 28)

This legislation provided the first glimpse at a form of public schooling for African children in Cincinnati at public expense. This act was followed by more legislation which provided that the new public schools for the Africans be self-governed by black male property owners in the community. "In other words, colored people, through representatives of their choice, would have the [sic] spend public funds, choose teachers and decide curriculum" (Macke, 1999, p. 29). The representatives were not totally of their choice as African women were automatically eliminated by default. This legislative provision allowed for the choosing of six black trustees for the initiation of two African school districts.

White Community members along with the white school board clearly opposed such state legislative actions. The local school board adamantly opposed blacks controlling any schools due to, among other things, the widespread belief of white moral and intellectual superiority (Macke, 1999). In their view, Africans were simply inferior and unfit to have educational leadership roles—even regarding their own children. The white school board resisted the protest by blacks for almost a year; this was spearheaded by Peter Clark, John Gaines, and the new trustees attorney, Flamen Ball. "The case was contested by the city officials, even in the Supreme Court, which decided against the officious whites" (Woodson, excerpt in Dabney, 1926, p. 44).

Thus, with Supreme Court backing, 4 teachers (three black, one white) and the rented rooms in two churches, the process of educating African children had begun only to be thwarted after three months of operation as the City Treasurer continuously refused to release the school's funding of $2,177.62. After appealing to the School Board on the issue, the board passed a resolution of "having no control" over the City Treasurer on the matter and declined to interfere. A week later the Board voted to "respectfully suggest and recommend that the City pay the teachers and the rent (total of $204.50) out of humanitarian good will" (Macke, 1999, p. 35). Clearly, bending to the will of a strong anti-African, white supremacist force, by 1853 the Ohio Assembly had repealed the Act of 1849, and the Africans in Cincinnati had lost the minuscule control of their schools to the local white School Board.

This "topsy-turvy" struggle of black resistance to white domination yielded, for a short time, the re-transferring of the control of black schools into the hands of the black board of trustees. Although the record is not clear on how long it took for the African people to wrestle control of their schools from the white community and School Board members, there is clarity in the fact that by 1874 "the colored board was abolished never to be re-established" (Shotwell 1902 excerpt in Dabney, 1926, p. 108).

Now, with the black school board abolished in 1874, "and in 1887, when the Arnett law went into force, separate colored schools as a class were abolished, for the law now permitted colored children to attend schools for whites. . . The results need hardly be told" (p. 108). By this time, the record seems clear that some African people were going to stay in Cincinnati and fight for equality and justice with new access to white public schools. At the same time it also seems clear that as early as the 1850s, other blacks were looking for "a better kind of freedom."

To the tune of "Oh, Susanna" one African man fleeing slavery but also experiencing the unsafe world of Ohio in the mid-nineteenth century wrote,

> Ohio's not the place for me;
>   For I was much surprised
> So many of her sons to see
>   In garment of disguise.
> Her name has gone throughout the world,
>   Free Labour, Soil and Men—
> But slave had better far be hurled
> Into the Lion's Den.
>
> Farewell, Ohio!
> I'm not safe in thee;
> I'll travel on to Canada
> Where colored men are free. (Macke, 1999, p. I)

Throughout the remainder of the 19th century battles of this nature continued yielding black victories followed by white backlash in a continuous effort to keep Africans in "free" Cincinnati "in their place." Although the first constitution of the state of Ohio in 1802 upheld the 1787 national Ordinance that prohibited slavery in the area, it seems clear that the level of African/black subordination to European/whites remained prevalent. Even from the mid-to-late nineteenth century, many of the Cincinnatian authorities were unable to "practice what was put on paper." Reflecting on the various European groups and their varying temperaments toward Africans in Cincinnati, it seems as though anti-Africanist sentiments were clearly the most forceful. Africans, along with the help of more progressive, abolitionist oriented, European/white groups seemed unable to hold sway against other anti-African white groups on long-term substantive policy issues at both the state and local levels.

Nevertheless, late nineteenth century Cincinnati, in many ways, represented the first taste (although bitter-sweet) of possible freedom for many enslaved Africans considering the "slave state" status of neighboring Kentucky during the pre-Civil War era. Nevertheless, for Africans of any time period during the 1800s, the magic wand of crossing the Ohio River often times presented quite grim forms of social and political oppression and subordination. According to Macke (1999):

> For much of the 19th century free black residents of Ohio lived as a caste, in a social and political purgatory, dangling precipitously between bondage and citizenship, on a line controlled by white civic elites. In order to cross this dark abyss, black residents had to have the political support of influential white citizens but, more importantly, they needed the strength to slowly and laboriously pull *themselves* across. (p. I; italics mine)

For, as the early and late migrations of Africans from the south to northern parts of the country were not absent of the white supremacy temperament of the day—a general American temperament of socially constructed whiteness over blackness be it in a northern liberal or a southern conservative nature. John Malvin alluded to this forceful white supremacy temperament in a northern state proclaiming,

> I thought coming to a free state like Ohio, that I would find every door open to receive me, but from the treatment I received by the people generally, I found it little better than Virginia. I found that every door was closed to the colored man in a free state except the jails and penitentiaries. . . . (Macke, 1999, p. 8; Malvin, 1879, p. 11-12)

The historical contextualization of African-Americans throughout the nineteenth century helps in putting into focus blacks and education throughout the twentieth century in the city of Cincinnati, and similar continuing struggles facing blacks at the beginning of the twenty-first century. It must be noted that by the turn of the twentieth century, the fight for just educational opportunities was by no means over. The Arnett Law of 1887 had provided the legislative means to African access of tax funded public education, but as history has clearly demonstrated, public policy doesn't easily erase the socialized contempt and hatred created over generations of irrational privilege and prosperity. For just a few years earlier in *The Independent Weekly* of New York, Frank Quillan reported, "Samuel J. Tilden, Democratic candidate for the presidency in 1876, called Ohio a "d----d" nigger state"" (excerpt in Dabney, 1926, p. 74).

Chapter 2

Cincinnati, Blacks, and Education in the 20th Century

> Samuel J. Tilden, Democratic candidate for the presidency in 1876, called Ohio a "d----d" nigger state.
>
> —Frank Quillan,
> *The Independent Weekly* of New York

Frank Quillan (1905) addressed the continued pervasiveness of race prejudice in Cincinnati as a Ph. D. candidate in the history department at the University of Michigan. Quillan's early twentieth century perspective on race in Cincinnati provides insights into the social climate of the city, a climate to which the arena of education is intricately interwoven. For even in the light of legislative policy mandating blacks be educated in the same schools as whites, after exploring Quillan's observations of this era, one must ponder the humanness of white/black interaction in the schools during this epoch.

By 1905, no colored man had been allowed to enroll in the University of Cincinnati's Medical College or any other facility of medical training in the city. In reference to African men, Quillan highlights the fact that:

> If he leaves the city and secures his training elsewhere and then comes back again, he finds the door of opportunity closed. The colored doctor, no matter what his training has been or what his ability and standing may be, is not allowed to operate in the large City Hospital, a public institution maintained by taxation to which the colored people contribute their share. (Dabney, p. 74)

Furthermore, blacks reluctantly treated in segregated wards of the public City Hospital were not given the opportunity to be treated by another African person, as black employment in the public facility was non-existent.

From an ethical standpoint, one has to reflect on the efficacy of public schooling institutions during this era. This type of reflection becomes even more imperative considering the treatment of blacks when it came to the more dangerous occupations of the city like firefighting. Quillan reported, "There is not a Negro to be found in the city fire department, which employs hundreds of men, all, of course, paid out of public taxation. The reason given for their absence is that white firemen will not work with them. . . ." (p. 74). The Municipal Bath House, Mechanics' Institute (probably the largest of its kind in the state), popular parks such as Chester, The Lagoon, and Coney Island were "off limits" to Africans. Blacks were also denied access to restaurants and hotels—they were simply off limits. "The Bartenders' Union has passed a resolution forbidding its members to wait on a colored person. . . ." (p. 75). Even the black established Y.M.C.A. was forced to change its name to the Y.B.C.A.—with the B indicating "Boys." Thus, just how warm could the public schools be, now that they were opened to all by the Arnett Law some fifteen years earlier? A large portion of the answer lies in this assertion by Quillan, "Not one is employed as a teacher in the public schools. . . ." (p. 77).

Nevertheless, few Africans had been able to participate in postal work, and a small number had become proficient in the learned professions of law, ministry, and medicine for the benefit of helping other Africans. Interestingly, Quillan shared his perspective on the causes of all that he had observed in the city of Cincinnati stating, "The one big cause is that—well, *just* BECAUSE" (p. 77). White supremacy/racism was, and still is, simply irrational from the point of view of the oppressed, yet a seemingly rational organization of social reality for their oppressors.

Along with the irrational "well, *just* BECAUSE" race based finding, Quillan also shares other findings on the virulent race prejudice in Cincinnati in the early 1900s. One finding was that whites typically viewed the blacks coming from the South as ignorant and seeking their (the whites) land in addition to wanting the same rights as the whites. Quillan also found that the city newspapers always emphasized race when reporting on a crime committed by an African person. There were headlines that read "A Big Black Burly Brute of a Negro" does such and such and the whole race gets a share of the blame (excerpt in Dabney, p. 77). Race was usually not mentioned in connection to newspaper articles reporting white crimes. Regarding attitude, Cincinnatians seemed to emulate the South, especially those white Cincinnatians who had visited the slave South and witnessed first hand the barbaric treatment of the enslaved Africans. Quillan states, "It is almost the universal observation that such people, after their return, forever despise the Negro" (pp. 77-78). White people constantly viewed blacks as undependable, lazy, shiftless, and prone to thievery. Finally, Quillan's research revealed the whites dislike of blacks entering politics and demanding rewards for their community. Blacks were running for public offices and this sense of African self-determination engendered much resentment by the whites who felt superior to blacks—even the poorest whites in the city (Dabney, 1926). With a few exceptions, Frank Quillan's observations still linger contemporarily.

Living in shabby rundown tenements known today as The West End (not to be confused with the West Side) poor Africans continued to strive for a better life against "persistent racial segregation, poverty, and political marginalization. . . . In the 1930s and 1940s, the West End was the site of the first public housing project in Cincinnati funded by the Public Works Administration: Laurel homes and the neighboring Lincoln Court Homes" (Gaston, Kelley, Knight-Abowitz, Rousemanaire, & Solomon, 1999, p. 1). Curiously, neighboring the two housing projects sits the central Cincinnati police station whose charge is both to serve and protect.

In further historicizing the African people's situation throughout the mid-to-late twentieth century, Gaston et al' (1999) appeal to statistics stating,

> Census statistics tell part of the story. In the 40 years following 1950, the percentage of Cincinnatians who were African-American more than doubled, from 15 percent in 1950 to 38 percent in 1990. Of the city's white population in 1990, 44 percent of whites attend some sort of higher education, as compared with only 27 percent of African-Americans. Cincinnati is a city of neighborhoods, and these neighborhoods work to further define the ethnic and economic segregation of the city. Poor African-American families living in the poorest neighborhoods. . . . (Gaston et al., 1999, p. 3)

They go on to reveal some facts that if not put into historical perspective might be seen as startling adding, "today, the West End remains a primarily poor, African-American community. According to the 1990 census, 67 percent of families in West End lived below the poverty line, 76 percent of families were female-headed. . . ." (p. 4). The public, tax funded institutions of the city have, throughout its history, barred these people from the benefits and privileges due them based on their tax contributions. The statistics above should not be startling to anyone who has ventured to take a cursory look at the city's history and race relations. The Africans, historically saturated close to this area, simply never had a chance.

The African-American population in Greater Cincinnati/The Tri-State has grown exponentially with post-civil rights housing mobility to historically non-black areas of the city. However, the post 1950's era appears to be a microcosm of the state of Ohio in general when historicizing the issue of African-Americans and education. Furthermore, in broader perspective, the acknowledgment of disparities between wealthier and poorer school districts brought the issue of socio-economic class along with race into clearer focus during this era. The current system of public education's funding policies have been called into question by a multi racial/ethnic contingency of Ohioans for not only discriminating against the disenfranchised racial/ethnic groups but poorer school districts where even whites in the area attend as well. The system also seems to discriminate against taxpayers all over the state by putting varying loads of taxes against them to support an inequitable public education in their communities. These are problems germane to Greater Cincinnati.

Public school funding and finance has sparked a great deal of controversy. Public outcry on this issue became pervasive in December of 1991 after The Ohio Coalition for Equity & Adequacy of School Funding leveled a lawsuit against the state's school funding system. This group consisted of 587 of the state's 611 school districts all coming together as a coalition. The issue initiated much discussion on decrepit and sub-par schooling conditions for many students around the state. By July of 1994, Perry County Common Pleas Judge, Linton Lewis Jr., had ruled the state system unconstitutional, and by 1997, the Ohio Supreme Court had upheld Justice Lewis's orders for a total overhaul of the schools' funding system that would provide "thorough and efficient" schooling opportunities for every child in the state. Unfortunately, as the years have gone by, substantive change in Cincinnati's public schools has been a grindingly slow process making the city a prime target for the "hot" voucher initiatives currently being explored in other places in the state and around the country.

After exploring Frank Quillan's 1905 observations of racial issues in the city and the growing school funding and finance dilemma affecting poorer whites as well, *Race In Cincinnati*, a report commissioned by The Stephen H. Wilder Foundation, was published in 1994. The reporters of this study wasted no time as the first line of page one reads, "Racism *is alive and well* in Cincinnati" (p. 1; italics mine). This study revealed several key insights into the general social relationships of Cincinnatians in which the educational system is a microcosm of the ills that beset both blacks and the city of Cincinnati.

In the midst of the city's professional baseball team owner Marge Schott, sharing with the world that she had a "million dollar nigger" (referring to an African-American player on her team) and the now yearly erection of the Ku Klux Klan's cross in the city's Fountain Square, the report highlights,

> . . . African-Americans generally perceive whites as having greater advantages in life and as being "sheltered from most of life's difficul-ties". Meanwhile, white respondents perceive a significantly lower sense of work ethic among blacks. Both races, however, strongly agree that white families envision a brighter future for their children than black families. (p. 1)

The polarization of life perceptions by those identified as either black or white in the study seem to be a typical reaction of this country on issues of this nature. Another example of this phenomenon could also be wit-nessed after the polls were released on the guilt or innocence of O.J. Simpson in the recent so-called "trial of the century;" while looking at the same televised trial, blacks overwhelmingly voted innocent and whites overwhelmingly guilty.

As of April of 2001, in the same month as I write this manuscript, the city of Cincinnati has gained international attention for a rebellion (some refer to the situation as thugs rioting) in the city stemming from the killing of an unarmed black nineteen year old male by a white police officer. The city has been declared in a state of emergency, and the mayor to curtail the rebellion, protesting, and looting has initiated a citywide curfew—everyone in by eight! It is as though the 1994 *Race in*

Cincinnati report could have predicted this ominous state of affairs. In outlining the perspectives of blacks the study stated,

> . . . we can say safely that blacks in the city see racism as a much bigger problem than whites. Blacks are much more concerned about areas where they feel they are not treated fairly. They have strong perceptions of white people having advantages or privileges that they do not have. And they feel that whites are not terribly interested in talking about racism or seeing things change. (Simurda, 1994, p. 21)

In another of the study's findings, Simurda alludes to whites asserting,

> Whites, on the other hand, see a problem with a much smaller scope and are not as clear about its source. They see racism as less pervasive than blacks. And they indicate that blacks need to work harder in order to overcome any disadvantages they might have. While they acknowledge those disadvantages and some of the other effects of racism, they are not particularly interested in taking responsibility for them. (p. 21)

Simurda's study seems to highlight the white privilege that many researchers have studied and documented (see, Macintosh 1989, Delgado & Stefancic 1997). The recent racially motivated unrest in the city surely, and partly, stems from the attitudes of Cincinnatians identified at the beginning of the nineteenth century as well as the twentieth century's closing.

Bearing in mind the historical treatment of African-Americans in education and in general throughout the history of The Tri-State/Greater Cincinnati, independent schools, religious and secular community based initiatives have always been considered and implemented. The Marva Collins Preparatory School, created in 1990, is perhaps one of the latest educational manifestations created, operated, and attended overwhelmingly by African-Americans in the city. It is an institution brought into existence as a result of the turbulent historical relations of various groups in this place called Cincinnati.

Chapter 3

The Birth of MCPSC

The school's lead-teacher for the newly opened higher grades boarding campus, Mrs. Huff-Franklin, arrived for her first interview hoping to become a pioneer by embarking on a new and exciting educational opportunity in the city of Cincinnati. Even the stories of her first interview help to shed light on the birth of the school. The poignant memories of Dr. Mims, the school's President/CEO sitting behind an old tiny desk firing probing questions during the interview process. The school's lead-teacher had seen the inner sanctums of the city's educational system as a public schools employee for three years prior to her interview for this exciting new position. She had worked in some of the better funded as well as some of the more decrepit city public schools during that tenure. Nevertheless, Mrs. Huff-Franklin finds it hard to contain her laughter when she compares the humble church basement beginnings of MCPSC with the city's public schooling facilities. At the least, and even with all of their inadequacies, the city's public schools in which she had previously worked did have a "school building" to call their own. The basement of Mt. Olivet Baptist Church was where those integral in the creation of MCPSC first called home.

Bearing in mind all of the aforementioned, which could easily be perceived as shortcomings and weaknesses by an employee searching for a fresh, new teaching opportunity, Mrs. Huff-Franklin does not hesitate in making clear a different and rather honorable perspective. She takes great pride in sharing, "but it just didn't matter to me because I . . . I just felt like . . . I'm going to get in on this and I'm going to help in whatever way . . . you know . . . I'm going to do what I can to make it work. . . . And so that was just kind of the feel, it was almost like not so much coming into school just to teach children, but it was almost like a business I wanted to help see grow. . . ." And, help see the school grow is exactly what she did as she is currently the school's most tenured faculty member.

Within the school's first school year, the school's lead-teacher vividly remembers the rapidity of growth that took place. Although many private schools are known for their "weeding" process through selectively admitting and not admitting students for various reasons, MCPSC accepted whoever was willing to come. Mrs. Huff-Franklin also shared with a tone of humor yet filled with candor, "when you are starting out, you can't be picky. . . ." That statement was quickly followed up with more clarification as to the school's early realities as many of the school's first students came lacking many of the school-readiness skills needed for success. Mrs. Huff-Franklin shared, "that's most of the people we had because nobody generally comes to something new that they are unsure of unless their child has had so much failure elsewhere. . . ." MCPSC simply opened its doors to anyone who believed in the Marva Collins Method and trusted that this new educational endeavor could prove successful if given a chance.

With the school's first year underway, Mrs. Huff-Franklin took on the responsibilities of teaching a multi-aged class consisting of the first thru the fourth grade. While discussing the topic she exclaimed, "I had them all!—with the exception of the other teacher who worked with pre-kindergarten." This multi-aged class consisted of approximately forty-three students during the school's first year. By the next year, the school's student population had more than doubled and gained a few more teachers. Now, Mrs. Huff-Franklin did not have to teach each grade level. So in that right, every year has become easier and easier through perseverance and the fact that as Mrs. Huff-Franklin puts it, "I started at the bottom (her voice deepens with emphasis on "the bottom").

Shouldering the Burden

The school's lead-teacher does not hesitate in sharing that every year following the school's opening things have gotten progressively better. She attributes her feelings to the fact that, "we started out so rough." But, in the next sentence she clarifies her sentiments and sheds more light on the joys and pains of the school's initial years, "but it was not rough because I was so excited (getting excited as she speaks) that we we're going to make this work . . . because you felt like everything was on your shoulders but it wasn't a burden, it was excitement. . . ."

After attending the training sessions at Westside Preparatory School, the world renown and first ever school created by Mrs. Marva Collins, the Marva Collins Preparatory School of Cincinnati's teachers had experienced the teaching techniques used to provide a solid education for children growing up in urban Chicago. Mrs. Huff-Franklin adds even more context to the joys and pains of MCPSC's initial years sharing,

> After we went to Mrs. Collins' training, we saw what she did . . . you were able to say well "if she did it in the ghetto and we're not in the ghetto!" (her voice raises) . . . you know our kids aren't going to be that rough, they had to go to uniforms because the gangs were ripping the clothes off the kids as they walked to school . . . they took their gym shoes . . . you know and things of that nature in Chicago. So, we're looking at it as, we don't have it that bad. . . . We can make this work . . . and that's why to me every year has been better and better because I started with no books (stressing no books) . . . totally no books. . . . And then we didn't even have a copier machine . . . and you know, so much we didn't have so every year we obtained something else . . . and now we're in this building (referring to the new higher grades boarding campus) . . . you know carpet! (her voice raises as she laughs) books for every subject . . . and somebody to teach science, somebody to teach math and I'm not teaching it all. . . . And it's with that appreciation whereas maybe some would be complaining so much, I remember virtually having nothing . . . with the worst set of kids . . . and under the worst predicaments because we were in the basement of a church and every Friday we had to help break partitions down so it could go back to Sunday school for church. Then Monday building back up . . . you know . . . physically doing work. . . . But we did it because we had a goal and, Mrs. Mims saw this from day one (referring to the new higher grades boarding school campus). . . . Therefore, we had a goal that we were working towards. . . . Now the goal is a new goal and we're trying to have this International Boarding School. So, the goals just get higher and expand more and more each year. . . .

These are profound words from one of the school's dedicated lead-teachers.

Understanding the Mission

A school's mission statement represents that essential directive of group cohesion. I agree with Carl Glickman when he claims,

> Any successful organization, whether it is a community or a religious, social, business, or educational group, has a set of core beliefs that holds its individual members together. That set of beliefs transcends any one person's self-interest. In the long run, the core beliefs help the group accomplish its mission and fulfill the needs and aspirations of individuals. (1993, p. 15)

Thus, in an attempt to understand The Marva Collins Preparatory School of Cincinnati (MCPSC), it becomes imperative that we begin with an elaboration of its mission. The school's mission statement provides the initial compass bearings, which lead to further insights. The Marva Collins mission statement as of the creation of this manuscript reads as follows:

MISSION STATEMENT

The Marva Collins Preparatory School is a non-sectarian school based on the Marva Collins philosophy of education, which seeks to develop within each child the ability to think critically and to communicate feelings and ideas freely and effectively.

The Marva Collins Preparatory School, its governing board, its administration staff, teachers, and parents seek to establish an academic and social environment conducive to academic and moral development.

The Marva Collins Preparatory School is a scion of Westside Preparatory in Chicago, and is characterized by its dedication to the pursuit of academic excellence and ethical principles.

The Marva Collins Preparatory School believes that goals can only be achieved through academic programs implemented by a dedicated faculty, supportive parents and moral leaders.

The Marva Collins Preparatory School seeks to perpetuate a universal awareness through the study of diverse cultures and religions.

The Marva Collins Preparatory School believes in the empowerment of parents by eliminating professional elitism.

The Marva Collins Preparatory School seeks to change negative and impulsive behavior to positive and rational behavior.

January of 1990 marked the collective stirring of ideas by several concerned African-American citizens to create a more viable and effective educational opportunity for American children in the city of Cincinnati. In the same month, these concerned citizens, all aware of and interested in the Marva Collins philosophy and approach to education, established the school's first board of trustees and secured permission from Mrs. Marva N. Collins for the usage of her name in identifying their brainchild. By March of that same year, The Marva Collins Preparatory School of Cincinnati (MCPSC) had been incorporated as an independent school. All executive board members resigned by July of the same year with the exception of Cleaster Mims, the first board's secretary, who then became its President/CEO on July 17, 1990. The first group of executive board members resigned to move forward with the project and dismantled due to diversionary issues with Mrs. Marva Collins on the school's philosophy and initial direction. On October 1, 1990, with the consultation of Mrs. Collins of Westside Preparatory in Chicago, Mrs. Mims along with three teachers, parents, and members of Olivet Baptist Church opened the school's doors to provide a form of education to grades Kindergarten through sixth in the church's basement.

During this period Mrs. Mims nearing retirement at local Western Hills High, a city public school, was perceptive enough to recognize the future fate of Cincinnati's public educational system and the ramifications for the children being served in that system. For, some seven years after the opening of MCPSC, the Ohio Supreme court had ruled the state public school system of funding and finance (heavily based on local property taxes) unconstitutional stating that all students in the state were not receiving the resources necessary to provide a thorough and efficient public education. On numerous occasions of conversation at MCPSC, the now, Dr. Mims, has voiced her thoughts on the issue. In her office, she once shared with me "the public school system in this city is a sinking ship . . . and the charter schools that are popping up are nothing but rafts with holes in them," drawing on her Titanic metaphor. These sentiments clearly highlight her position in reference to the city's public and charter school institutions.

By the opening of the 1994 school year, MCPSC had made a transition from the church's basement to a circular architecturally styled building, a former European-American Jewish owned Yeshiva in the Roselawn neighborhood of Cincinnati. Vivid recollections of early impressions of the facility resurface as I spent many days as a fledgling college intern at the school during the fall of 1995. The building seemed to be small for a school as I drove up in the early mornings of September, the beginning stage of my internship that year. Yet the building's circular design with its classes on the circumference always seemed to distort my sense of direction making the place seem quite large once inside. From an aerial view, the building is probably reminiscent of a miniature U.S. Pentagon building with its five sharp edges smoothly chiseled away. I always found myself going the long route of the school's circular hallway in attempting to reach any destination in the building. There seemed to be no north, east, south or west when in the building, just locations on the circumference of the circular hallway.

With the classrooms situated around the circumference, the dining area was located in the center of the school. Actually, the dining area became multipurpose in the fall of 1995, becoming both the dining area and the 7/8th grade classroom. This structural change was implemented when the city fire codes' Marshal inspected the school and threatened to shut the building down the next day if changes had not been made upon his arrival the next day. There were few minor changes but the major change was the 7/8th grade classroom, which the Marshal had judged overcapacity. I clearly remember the determination and pride I felt that day as the President/CEO and the lead-teacher (then my supervising teacher) seemed unaffected by the threat of being shut down. We interns and the staff all stayed until after dark that evening rearranging the dining area into the new 7/8th grade classroom.

The next day, the inspector returned as promised finding the school in compliance meeting all of his specifications. My reflections are poignant as these seemingly "nitpicky," microscopic type inspections continue even at the new upper-grades boarding facility contemporarily. The staff at MCPSC clearly felt that the "powers that be" did not want an endeavor of this nature to succeed in 1995. Although never specifically identified, seemingly systematic, these same "powers that be" in many ways still make for similar sentiments some 5 years later. Comments to the tone of "it's always something" referring to some code violation in the new boarding campus building or "we know they are watching us" have been heard on occasions throughout the year. Putting the whole situation in perspective the President/CEO typically exclaims, "But they can't stop us, because it's not even about us, this is God's work . . . and they can't stop that—now can't they"? This seems to be a one-answer question in her mind—for who has the power to destroy an endeavor commissioned by God?

Despite bureaucratic roadblocks, the future looks bright as the doors for the school's higher grades boarding facility opened in September of 2001. This year marks the separation of MCPSC into two campuses—the lower grades (pre-k – 3rd) and higher grades (4th – 8th) Cleaster Mims International campuses. The higher grades boarding campus is located in Silverton, one of the affluent socioeconomic Central Suburb communities in the city. Exploring the motives behind the opening of The Cleaster Mims International Boarding School campus Dr. Mims states,

> We decided to start the boarding school because of the requests we have gotten from people across the state and across the nation asking that we establish a Marva Collins Preparatory School in their cities. . . . Establishing schools in all of those cities is physically impossible, but establishing a boarding school for people from other cities and around the world is possible. . . . Boarding schools help children build discipline, responsibility, self-reliance and independence. African-American youngsters especially need to develop responsibility, discipline and respect for themselves and others (Shoppers Guide for Community-Based Businesses, 2000, p, 16)

On other occasions, such as a school promotional video created through the efforts of the school's board, she adds more context to the reasoning behind the need of a boarding facility and contends that:

> . . . The idea came because we had a number of children who started with Marva Collins School and we lost them back to what I call "their environment." We thought with those children if we could just have had a place to keep them . . . all day, evenings and they did not have to go back to their neighborhoods, we could have saved more children. (Marva Collins Promotional Video, 1996)

In the end, I am assured, based on experiences at MCPSC, that this educational community has even more good and valid reasons for embarking on such an endeavor. An endeavor that even an optimist such as

I thought was far-fetched five years ago when the school's President took me and another intern to the then for-sale boarding school site and shared her future plans with us as interns. Who would have thought that I would be writing a book about the very building that I had, in my own mind, relegated ready for the demolition crew just five years earlier? Many of the building's windows were boarded up due to being broken by neighborhood vandals or "little punks" as the President/CEO referred to them in disgust at their wanton behavior. The grass was pretty high in places around the building. I mean, who would have known that just five years later this place would be refurbished and open for business?

MCPSC and CMIS are founded on the notions of instilling the values of academic excellence, self-esteem, self-reliance, self-determination, perseverance, integrity, and respect for self and others. These philosophical values are a part of the school's major four pronged agenda of schooling.

On Schooling the Children

Encapsulated in the school's agenda is the belief that books are windows to the world. Thusly, mainstream traditional trade books such as "See Spot Run . . . " are replaced by classics such as "The Odyssey" or Shakespeare's "Macbeth." For, the lead-teacher is known for stressing the point, "why just teach children simple words like "big" when they could just as easily learn words such as "huge," "gargantuan," or "enormous?"" Therefore, at MCPSC an emphasis on strong vocabulary skills are of immense importance. The school's written agenda in reference to students at MCPSC is clear on its stance in reference to recess or "down time"—it should be nonexistent. The school's promotional brochure states, "Not one minute of valuable classroom time is wasted—there is no recess, and lunch is eaten at the desk."

Rhythm is an important aspect of schooling at MCPSC. Lessons should be performed in a sing-song fashion whenever possible—"this makes the lesson stick." Mrs. Townsel-Benson, the lead-teacher for the lower grades campus shares her belief that the children at MCPSC typically come from a rhythmic environment, surely alluding to the overwhelmingly African-American student population. Thus, the school's use of rhythm only taps into what is already "natural" for the students (Video, 1996).

Finally, MCPSC has dedicated itself as an educational institution to the principle of producing future leaders. And, as soon as a student enters the school they are inundated with a plethora of opportunities to verbally express themselves in public forums: such as their classrooms, weekend "Prepping for Power" showcases, and citywide performances. Thus, the ability to articulate ideas and communicate effectively in public settings is deemed central to the schooling process at MCPSC.

On Schooling the Educators

The school's promotional brochure "gets right to the point" in reference to teacher roles stating,

> Traditional teaching methods and education parameters don't apply here. There are no extra-curricular activities to take away from the reasons we're here—to learn. When a teacher comes to us from a public school or even from another private school, it takes time for them to learn our style. Every teacher must truly love these kids and be willing to buy in to our methods, or they don't teach at MCPSC. (MCPSC brochure)

On teachers and classroom size, the MCPSC agenda alludes to the notion of classroom size not being of paramount importance. On this agenda item, an old teaching cliché seems quite appropriate; "if you can teach five, you can teach one hundred five." In other archival material, documentation can be found in reference to ideally a 1:20 teacher-student ratio with teacher understudies and teacher assistants available. The teachers at MCPSC are charged to teach pride, allow no disciplinary problems, and accept no excuses for students not doing their best at all times.

On Schooling the Parents

As the third prong of the MCPSC schooling agenda, the aspect of schooling parents seems to be one of the battles of persuasion in which the faculty had to win after several years of getting the parents to buy into the school's philosophy and methods. The agenda states that parents must not harbor perceptions of powerlessness when it comes to making a "real difference" in the education of their children. Parents are expected to attend the school's Parent Meeting on the 2nd Saturday of each month during the school year. At these meetings, students' assignments for the month are to be collected by their parents in the child's classroom. Finally, an emphasis on the school/home dichotomy is expected to be understood by the parents as being inseparable. The MCPSC agenda states that the values taught and practiced in school should also be reinforced at home and everything the child does.

On Schooling the Public

The fourth and final prong of the MCPSC agenda is a bold statement of just what the school is and its purpose. The school's promotional brochure proclaims,

> We are truly non-conformists. Because our school does not operate according to the same "standards" as more traditional systems, new observers are skeptical when they experience our typical daily activities for the first time. Where most classrooms are quiet and subdued—not unlike the atmosphere of a library, ours are loud and boisterous—more like a songfest or a revival. Where other students may work individually at their desks, ours are often standing at the front of the room reciting verses form Shakespeare.

Schooling the public seems to be the one agenda item charged with finally setting the record straight on what this educational institution is and what it is all about. This is a school community that seems not to mind sharing its pride in what they consider and perceive to be a non-conformist approach to schooling.

Chapter 4

First Day of School at the "New" Cleaster Mims Campus

My day began by embarking on the fifty minutes to an hour drive, that was affected by the movement of traffic, into the city of Cincinnati. Little did I know at the time how invaluable this lengthy drive to and from the school would be; it helped me to both clear up and make better sense of my experiences during the year that I spent at MCPSC. I wanted to arrive at the school by 8:30 A.M. bearing in mind the school day began at 9:00 A.M. Early insights would be pivotal in understanding and getting a feel for the community's initial interactions, especially on the first day in a new school setting. None of the teachers had ever taught in this building nor had any of the students ever attended the school. Furthermore, many students never experienced any other physical school setting besides that of MCPSC's lower grades campus. However, some of the students in each grade had been a part of the MCPSC family since pre-kindergarten.

The school's President/CEO, Dr. Mims, had expressed to me a few nights earlier over the phone, that many technical things would have to be worked out in reference to the students starting school at the new facility. The new, higher grades boarding campus, unlike the much smaller, lower grades campus is a former Catholic nursing home. The building is two stories with approximately 105 rooms and a basement large enough to house the school store, all classrooms, and the school's dining area. The basement is, for the most part, where the actual day-to-day interactions of the school took place. Moreover, for the first day, many logistics were going to have to be worked out as the "rubber was about to meet the road" and the new school year was about to begin. I had volunteered countless hours to help renovate the building throughout the previous summer and wanted to do all that I could to make sure that the school was off and rolling on the first day.

As I turned onto the private street approaching the new higher grades boarding campus on that cool and misty fall morning, the first thing that I noticed was a newly built nursing home. The modern looking nursing home sat next door to the much older and stoic looking former nursing home that is now the higher grades boarding campus. The two structures, separated by about 60 yards and a row of newly planted hedges clearly showed which building is the elder. The older building, now known as The Cleaster Mims International Boarding Campus, is the very large two-story red brick building. Its grass was now nicely cut and the weeds and bushes were neatly trimmed which provided a pleasant image of a physical structure no longer abandoned.

I usually entered by way of the streets that led to the back of the school. Construction crewmember cars and company trucks were still parked outside the building. These were the same cars that were in the parking lot during those hot summer days when I drove down to help paint and clean the interior of the building as a volunteer.

I can recall earlier in the summer during the month of July talking with one of the construction workers, an African-American male who appeared to be in his mid-to-late twenties. He was very enthusiastic about the school's opening and the fact that African-American students would be the primary student population attending this institution. He obviously admired the school's President/CEO, as I would hear him inquiring about the school as though he was an interested parent when they had conversations. When he conversed with Dr. Mims and the other elder African-American women who volunteered during the summer, he never forgot to say "yes maam" or "no maam" symbolically humbling himself as a gesture of respect.

Even in his great excitement over the possibilities and potential of the school, the construction worker thought that it would be a stretch to assume that the school would be ready to open in early September, just about two months away. I recall sharing his sentiments with the President/CEO of the school assuming that as one of the workers who saw the building plans daily, who would have known better than he when the facility would be ready for operation. She promptly dismissed the notion and asserted, "that's his problem, he has a limited vision."

What MCPSC's President/CEO promptly dismissed as a lack of vision was a profound indication of her strong convictions and visionary capabilities. Sometimes her visions seemed quite unrealistic to the optimistic observer of some of her feats—even to those such as her husband who surely knew her better than most. To illustrate this point a particular experience during the summer before the opening of MCPSC is worth noting.

During the summer leading to the official opening of the higher grades boarding campus, the school President/CEO had plans to host and entertain over fifty guests who would be visiting from South Africa. The South Africans had invited MCPSC's students, staff, and parents to their country during the previous year and now it was their turn to reciprocate the gesture. The South African guests were to live at the boarding school campus during their visit, which seemed to be far from ready to house anyone during this stage in its renovations. Overall, the building was not up to the city's safety codes and it seemed as though far too many things needed to be done with far too little time. Many tasks had to be accomplished—electricians had to repair and replace light fixtures and wiring, beds needed to be assembled in some rooms, rooms had to be scraped and painted, carpet had to be laid in various areas and bathrooms needed plumbing and had to be scrubbed, just to name a few. The President/CEO's strategy was to get as many willing hands as possible: parents, friends, European-American sorority groups from her university, as well as the 20/20 program.[1] Her goal was to get one wing of the first floor ready to accommodate their guests. Just pulling that part of the plan off seemed unreasonable with only weeks before the guests were to arrive.

Standing to the back of the school during one of those laborious days of renovations, her husband and I both shared some laughs as we reflected on the feat that seemed impossible to both of us but not to his wife. He told me that his wife is both "strong minded and strong willed" and, as such, he and their only son who is now a practicing medical doctor, had come to the conclusion that to slow her down is to make her miserable. "All she know is how to go, go, go," he would say as we both laughed partly in confusion or shall I say shortsightedness of why she worked the way she did and partly in admiration of her undying will to

---

1. A program for juvenile delinquents doing court mandated community service hours.

see things through. She dreamed bigger than most and did not mind putting forth the effort to make things happen.

Her husband and I both seemed to privately agree that the boarding school building was in bad shape and maybe she should have invited the South Africans on a later date. Needless to say, and to our surprise (at least mine), by the time the South Africans arrived, the west wing of the building had passed all of the city safety code inspections. With brand new electrically illuminated emergency fire exit modules throughout the west wing halls signaling "come on in, its safe and ready," that portion of the building was prepared to receive their guests. I still puzzle over the level of planning, organizing, and directing that was necessary to pull off such a feat. I even heard some of the contracted, construction crewmembers speaking highly of the President/CEO in reference to the accomplishment.

Although travel did not allow me to witness and interact with the South Africans during their visit to MCPSC, upon my return and in-quiry, I learned how joyous the occasion had been. The chatter around the school was that the South Africans loved their stay and the hosts comprised of MCPSC's parents, staff, and students loved having a place where they could say, "come on in, we have a room for all of you."

If looking at this stoic, colossal structure (aged yet still looking to have at least another hundred years worth of life) from a bird's eye view, the building would resemble a block styled capital letter "E". As I ap-proached MCPSC on the first day, some of the windows in the upper stories of the building were still boarded and being repaired by construc-tion workers, because someone had vandalized several areas which made parts of the building still appear as if it were condemned.

I entered the school through the back door taking the stairs up to the chapel. I immediately noticed that the first floor of the building, where the chapel is located, was quiet, but the building was not empty as I also noticed classroom lights on down the hall in the basement. The two newly installed glossy wood doors that flapped open leading into the chapel immediately caught my attention. Clearly, this room had been designed as a part of the building architecture for worship services for the elderly who formerly occupied the building when it was a Catholic nursing home. The windows to the right and left were stained cathedral style with pic-tures reflecting the themes of Roman Catholicism and symbols of the Crucifix. The chairs of assorted colors, some of which were the foldout metal types and others that would suit a dining room set, were parted down the center thus giving clear view to the slightly elevated pulpit area.

MCPSC's first day of school started in the chapel. I returned to the chapel after wandering throughout the building admiring the west-wing and the newly painted walls in the basement. I heard the school's back door opening and slamming shut as well as the lead-teacher, Mrs. Huff-Franklin, directing parents and students to the chapel for the morning's assembly. Students exiting the buses had already filed into the chapel, directed by other teachers as they chatted with old classmates, gazed at their new assembling area, and helped one another straighten out neckties and fold down shirt collars.

Some MCPSC parents who seemingly were happy to accompany students in the chapel on their first day of school sat at the back of the room as the students were all directed to sit in their appropriate sections, which were marked by grade levels with their new teachers who stood by the grade level markers. Class section demarcations in the chapel were some of the first structures created at MCPSC, and they gave the students a sense of direction, at least for the first ritual of the day. I took the end seat on the front row of the room and attempted to model what I knew the teachers would want the students to do as they entered.

The first morning of school opened with the lead-teacher requesting that one of the larger, older looking, fully uniformed girls lead the school in prayer. The girl asked all students, staff, and others to bow their heads as she chose to recite *The Lords Prayer*, a prayer taken from The Bible. Afterwards, a chorus of individuals joined her in the concluding "Amen." Morning prayer was to be a daily ritual, which meant that the conception of God would be central at MCPSC.

The lead-teacher moved into action by welcoming everyone and then focused attention on explaining the new MCPSC morning routine structure—coming in quietly and an opening prayer were givens with no need for reiteration. She gave directions to a room of students who would not know where to go or what to do if released into their new school environment. With a quick signal to the other teachers, they began to distribute copies of the morning poems including the Marva Collins Creed. Many students declined to take the papers indicating that they already had everything committed to memory. In the midst of this minor commotion the lead-teacher signaled the students to rise chorus style to recite the creed with her assuming the directress role. She asserted, "We will start with The Creed. . . . go!" The students all in unison began with a recital of The Creed.

During this impressive recital, I noticed many students loosening up as the words of The Marva Collins Creed rang familiar after the summer break. Some students added hand and body gestures at key moments that they remembered from previous years. Others spent time peering around trying to become acquainted with the new environment. While others even peeked onto their neighbor's paper realizing that they should have accepted a copy of The Creed the teachers distributed moments ago.

Without hesitation, the students transitioned directly to another poem—an indicator that there were many returning MCPSC veterans in the room. Maltbie Davenport Babcock's poem entitled, "Be Strong" appealed to the school's strong work ethic, which is a valuable and honorable MCPSC trait. In unison once again came a loud, "Be Strong by Maltbie Davenport Babcock . . . we are not here to play, to dream, to drift. . . ."

Following Maltbie Davenport Babcock's poem, the entire school transitioned to the final poem of the morning entitled, "A Great Somebody by Adrienne Sealy Hardesty". By this time, the lead-teacher had begun distributing copies of the speeches to new students and those returning veterans who were not participating and had declined copies earlier, so that they could begin to both read and recite with the rest of the school. It was becoming obvious which students did not know the words or had the recitations committed to memory. Some students were seemingly suffering from "if you don't use it you loose it" indicative of not constantly practicing these poems at home over the summer. The next poem had started, "I am a serious child. . . . I am a serious child with serious goals. . . ."

The poem was a great self-esteem booster as the students both read and recited the lines in a personal manner. At this point, the lead-teacher directed all students to have a seat. As the students seated themselves, silence filled the room, and she took advantage of the opportunity to reiterate that this morning's behavior is how students at Cleaster Mims International should behave every morning during whole school chapel time. As she continued with comments about student uniforms by calling exemplars to the front of the room where she stood, the President/CEO entered the chapel walking expeditiously with a strong sense of purpose straight down the center aisle toward the front and stood next to the lead-teacher. The lead-teacher halted her comments as she and the President/ CEO privately conversed.

Obviously, the conversation must have been one of "getting on the same page" in reference to the procedure for directing students to their new classes in an orderly manner. After nodding in agreement to the lead-teacher's inaudible lip movements, the President/CEO instructed parents after apologizing for arriving late due to getting the lower grades campus started this morning. She told them "I know that many of you parents have not been down in the basement area to tour the new school, but I am going to ask you all to wait in the chapel until the students and their teacher have been dismissed and are working in their new class-rooms. Then, I can take those of you who want to see the new school on a tour." Spur of the moment decisions of this nature characterized much of what happened at MCPSC throughout the school year. Flexibility, the ability to troubleshoot, and thinking quickly on your feet were necessary in such a new educational setting where structure was being created and re-created daily.

As I descended the stairs leading to the basement following the 5/6th grade students who had been instructed to walk in the middle of the hall in absolute silence, we turned and headed down the east wing of the basement; the students complied. As we entered the basement, I noticed that it was rather pleasing to my eyes. Long hours of work over the past year had rendered this place complete with all of the trappings of a tradi-tional modern school hallway. The walls were freshly painted in the two-tone lighter and darker beige that emanated a neutral and not-too-stimu-lating feel of a red or some other intense and vivid tone. The floor appeared to be both buffed and polished, which added a pleasing, "final touch" to the total ambiance needed for a walk down the hall on the first day of school in a new school building.

Straight ahead as we moved down the east wing of the hallway was the fourth grade classroom, which was about fifty yards down at the end of the hallway. The 5/6th graders in front of what appeared to be a rather long line veered left at the end of the hallway into the largest class of all—the lead-teacher's new "stomping grounds." If one veered to the right, one would head into the Spanish classroom, which was located at the opposite end of the hallway facing the 5/6th grade class.

As I stood toward the end of the long 5/6th grade line, not yet reach-ing the end of the hallway, I noticed a vacant room to the right, which with a tour of the basement this summer I was told would be the site of the future school store. Opposite the future school store is where the maintenance/cargo drop-off area is located; it is identifiable by a small painting beside the door indicating "Maintenance Area." Adjacent to the maintenance area are the girls and faculty's restrooms. As I walked further down the hall, keeping pace with those students walking quietly toward the back of the line and in the center of the hallway, I passed several vacant, unfurnished classrooms. Further, down the hallway to the right was the Science room followed by the 7/8th grade classroom, whereas the lab was across the hall.

All students entered the classroom and located their desks, which were designated by the name labels and positive phrases such as "Always Try My Best," "Be Strong," etc. By this time, I could hear the quiet commotion of the other classes beginning to enter and settle into their new classrooms prompting me to exit as the lead-teacher explained the school's locker room procedures. As I exited, the lead-teacher selected a small group of students to go into the locker room to choose a locker for the year. The locker room was filled with lockers behind the front wall of the 5/6th grade classroom.

Standing in the hallway, I could clearly hear all three teachers as they were the center of attention, and the students all sat quietly as if at attention on the first day of a military's basic training "boot camp." Each teacher's door was open as I could both hear and see the 7/8th grade teacher from the hallway sharing with his students their morning routine as they all focused on his tall, slim frame and South African accent.

> We will keep our things here with us until the other classes have gone to the locker room, then we will go. I am very excited to be here and cannot wait to get started with our school year. . . . How many of you had the opportunity to visit the schools in South Africa last year. . . ?

He continued talking sustaining the students' full attention as he paced up and down the three rows of desks that matched the neutral beige walls of the classroom and hallway.

I could also hear the fourth grade teacher asking questions and explaining classroom protocol. The seasoning and experience of enough years to retire from the city's public schools emanated from her voice as she talked to her students for the first time.

Keep all of your things beside your desks for right now . . . we will go
to the lockers when it is our turn, then you can put your things away. . . .
I expect everyone's attention when I am talking and no talking in our
class without permission . . . permission is granted by raising your
hand and being acknowledged by me . . . raise your hand if you already know The Creed by heart. . . ?

The school was "out of the gates" and a new year at the MCPSC
higher grades boarding campus was underway. This morning encom-
passed the type of energy created when the time finally came; everyone
was physically occupying the place, and space long talked about, dreamed
of, and imagined. The energy of the school felt exciting to me, like the
first day of vacation or orientation at summer camp or a trip abroad. This
school day represented in part the fulfillment of all of the work and effort
of those who had toiled to make this place an educational reality. The
school was "out of the gates."

Part II

Lessons of Wisdom

Chapter 5

The Wisdom of MCPSC Faculty

"Prepping for Power"

Prepping for Power is an event central to the character of The Marva Collins Preparatory School of Cincinnati. On Sunday afternoons throughout the year, the various grade levels at MCPSC get to "show what they know" through poetry, song, dance, speeches, and many other creative genres of expression to their families and the broader community. I find it useful to insert the words of Dr. Mims as she once shared with parents during a Prepping for Power showcase, a brief historical sketch which highlighted the rationale for such an event. The crowd sat quietly as she spoke:

> Prepping for Power is an activity that we at the Marva Collins School really believe in. This is an opportunity for our children to practice speaking in front of large crowds so that they will be prepared for some of the larger events that we have throughout the school year. . . . We at the Marva Collins School really work hard and want our children to be very articulate and verbal, as well as proficient in their writing skills. We believe in this very much because no matter how smart a child may be, if he or she can not articulate his or her ideas to others or are afraid to do so, then it really doesn't matter how smart they are—no one will know. This event is also an opportunity to build our students self-esteem and self-confidence. For, I am a speech instructor at a local university and I have seen adults freeze up in little classroom settings. Speaking in front of a group of people might just be the next scariest thing to death! So, we give our children a chance to

practice this vital skill so that they will be able to accomplish what they
will want to accomplish after leaving our school.

After performances, Dr. Mims would oftentimes share the school's
philosophy for engaging in Sunday evening "Prepping for Power" rituals, which approximately twice per semester called for commitments by
staff that stretched beyond the regular school week's responsibilities and
obligations. In her closing remarks she would highlight the benefits and
importance of realizing that MCPSC is a school community determined
to prepare leaders who will go out and accept the challenges of our world.
She once shared with the audience, "we want them to be able to stand
and speak in front of the President of the United States if called to do
so—or a legislator. We want them to be able to speak well and express
themselves so that when they go on to other institutions they will get the
role in a play or be selected for the chorus. I have watched many children
miss out on opportunities to perform in plays and other things because
they had to audition and could not win the roles that they wanted. Our
students will be prepared and will be able to make the cut."

Dr. Mims: Trying to Save the Children

An interview with Dr. Mims provides even deeper insight into this school
community. In this interview, she candidly shared thoughts on some
students who had to leave their school.

> . . . Well first of all, we found out from the parents that the children
> [referring to two boys who had attended the school] . . . I had a con-
> ference with them . . . and they would come into class and they would
> sleep . . . they would sleep all the time . . . and they wouldn't do any
> work. First of all, if attending Marva Collins you are going to
> work . . . or you don't eat . . . I mean just that. . . . We expect students
> to work and if they refuse to work, they will get put out of this school
> faster than if you had a fight . . . because if I think that you had a fight,
> because somebody stepped on your toe, it's an emotional thing, I can
> soothe that, I can work with you on that, I can try to change your
> behavior . . . but if you're just so stubborn that you're not going to
> work in order to learn . . . You are rebelling against knowledge itself
> and I'm not taking your parents money. . . . And so I tell them, you
> are wasting your parents money because you are not learning . . . not
> because they can't learn . . . It's because they refuse to learn.

Now I held on to (the two boys). . . . Their family will tell you that both of those boys made a 360 degree turn around in their attitude . . . but they were not coming from the place where academic learning was a joy for them . . . and when I talked with the parents about it, I found out that one of the reasons they were sleeping like they were . . . they were out at night smoking "pot" in the street with their neighbors. . . .

Now if I had the boarding school up and running, I probably could have taken those two boys and extended their day and I would have had them at the school and there would have been no "pot" smoking at night and no running out with the gang at night. . . . I may have been able to save those two boys.

But th-e-y were determined that they were not going to learn . . . that they were not going to do any work . . . and they just made sure that they did anything they could to keep from working . . . they didn't mind going outside picking up trash . . . but they were not going to learn. . . .

Stories such as the one above highlight just how complex it sometimes is to provide a good education at MCPSC. Not all stories have happy conclusions, yet I've never witnessed a school community that cared for children as those at MCPSC. Dr. Mims once shared, "I wish I had the money from the buckets of tears that I could have caught in my office. . . . If I had the gallon pails of tears and could trade them in for dollars . . . I would be rich." She was referring to the times when parents had sat in her office crying during conferences as their children struggled with school life. During the previously mentioned episode of the two brothers, the boys seemed to be quite nonchalant about the entire matter as their mother sat and cried in Dr. Mims' office. Dr. Mims adds more insights to the troubled boys situation stating:

. . . the mother (referring to the two boys above) sitting there weeping her eyes out while her sons sat nonchalantly with looks of unconcern . . . it had nothing to do with the school, it had nothing to do with the teachers. . . . He was just out there (now referring to the oldest of the two boys) . . . and the uncle was trying to save them . . . the mother couldn't afford to pay the money . . . the uncle was a retired man . . . and he was paying their school tuition.

. . . Now, some of these children I've been able to help but I looked at those two boys, they were too far gone. The dredges out there that was pulling them into those streets was stronger than the power I had to hold them . . . and I told them that . . . I told them that if I let go honey, it's over . . . because no one in the world is going to do for you what I've tried to do for you . . . but I said, you can change and you can come back when you're ready to do the work. . . . I mean that, I a-l-w-a-ys leave the door open for them.

The boys' mother instinctively felt as though her sons were headed on a path to jail, especially the eldest. She told him that day in Dr. Mims' office, with tears rolling down her cheeks, "you goin' to jail . . . that's all you gonna do. You keep gettin' older and older and you know that they're gonna put you in jail."

After leaving MCPSC shortly after that meeting, the boys were enrolled in a local public school. Dr. Mims phoned the boys' mother some weeks later to inquire about their progress and was informed that the oldest brother had been expelled from his new school. He had been sent to a juvenile delinquent program called 20/20 and not long after Dr. Mims was informed by his uncle that he was in "lock-up" at a juvenile facility. Her final words to me on the boys situation are very poignant. She shared, "I have done everything humanly possible. . . . It's like I've been saying . . . you're breaking my back now . . . I think that the only persons I've ever just let go was those two boys . . . but their environment, like I said . . . they were in a terrible, terrible, terrible environment . . . and the school couldn't overpower it."

Dr. Mims and Those Snakes

As the 2000-2001 school year progressed, I learned that sermon/lectures by Dr. Mims were not only crafted for students at MCPSC. Occasionally, while sitting in her office deliberating with a teacher over curricular matters in reference to team teaching the 7/8th grade class or conferencing with a parent, Dr. Mims would share philosophical insights slipping into sermon/lecture mode. These discussions always taught me something new about the school President/CEO's convictions. Below I attempt to provide the spirit of her famous sermon/lectures. She preached:

You see, we as a people have to get up off our butts and do something for ourselves—no one is going to give us anything for just sitting around and being lazy . . . that welfare system made many of our people that way, you know—especially in this city. In addition, we can't just keep blaming everything on racism, we know that there are poisonous snakes out there . . . but it doesn't mean that we have to spend all of our time hunting down the darn snakes. If you see a poisonous snake in your path, h-o-n-e-y you just go around it. Otherwise, by the time we spend all of our time chasing and trying to capture poisonous snakes, we could have done something for ourselves . . . you know what I mean . . . we can go on ahead and do some things for ourselves and stop sitting around blaming everything on racism and white folks.

These words of insight into Dr. Mims' understanding of racism as it exists in our society was met by nods of agreement as the teacher and I stood in her doorway while two parents sat in the office's newly furnished forest green, guest seats. The "snakes" seemed to symbolically represent deadly, poisonous (racist) individuals in our society.

Thus, if African-Americans in this society would carry on in their desires, aims, and goals with an understanding that, yes, there are snakes; but, do not spend an inordinate amount of time focused on snakes.

On another occasion but in the same vein of strong work ethic and self-sufficiency, Dr. Mims shared insights into her struggles of getting other African-Americans on the bandwagon in this mid-west city, as she and three 7/8th grade boys worked to shelve books in the developing library. She shared,

They just seem to think that everything is supposed to be handed to them, you know. H-o-n-e-y, we blacks from the south never acted like these people up here. We would get out and do what needed to be done; at least that's how I was raised down in the cotton fields of Alabama. But, nowadays I just don't understand our people. [She corrects herself] Well, I do understand them; they are just lazy and think that everything should be just handed to them—especially around here. We were just not brought up like that in the south. We were more like Booker T. (speaking of Booker T. Washington); we got out and did for ourselves. That's all I know!

Words of this nature echoed often. The "do for yourself attitude" and "that's all I know" approach to accomplishing goals kept Dr. Mims' "boat floating" during the times when seas were calm and afloat when the waters became turbulent—she could always count on herself. Furthermore, this was a lesson that she seemed to want all African-Americans to embrace.

Dr. Mims Speaks on Responsibility, Paying the Bills, and Good Eating Habits

During monthly Parent/Teacher meetings, Dr. Mims often had an opportunity educate MCPSC parents through her famous Sermon/Lectures. One particular meeting helps to elaborate her philosophy.

A Saturday Parent/Teacher Meeting

After the acknowledgement of summer volunteers, Dr. Mims transitioned to the issue of fundraising. "I want the children tuition bills paid this year . . . do you all understand what I am saying," were her first comments. She then went into a litany of directions on how to pay for the students' catered lunches. "Pay half, pay what you can . . . but pay something. I must pay the caterer each week, so I need that money from you even if you are not going to pay your child's tuition in full right then." She then told the story of a personal sacrifice she had made the prior summer to pay for insurance for the staff. "I had to pay three thousand dollars out of my own pocket because everyone's tuition was not up to par. And, believe me, I won't do it again because of delinquent tuition!" She ended this speech with a reminder for all of the parents, "always think about this institution and what part you play in whether it succeeds or fails."

> My staff's salaries are on the line here . . . it all rides on you all as parents doing the responsible thing, the correct thing. So, please pay your child's tuition because, you are either a part of the problem; tearing down this institution, or you are part of the solution; helping to make it prosperous. Always think in those terms about the livelihood of our school.

Finally, she opened the floor up to the parents for questions stating, "If you have any questions, the best person to ask is Dr. Mims. So, don't go and get it from the grapevine."

One African-American woman raised her hand and asked, "my child is not going to eat the lunch served at school and he comes home hungry complaining if I don't prepare his lunch. Can we have a fundraiser to help defray the catered lunch cost since I have to pay it in the tuition and my child's not going to eat it if he doesn't like it?" In response, Dr. Mims gave a speech about the past years when children would bring in very unhealthy lunches and the connections of that tendency to them performing well in school. In reference to the new boarding school campus, she also discussed her unwillingness to let students bring in lunches because of "the mess that was created" at the lower grades school with sour and spoiled food being found in various places in the school such as the students lockers and behind cabinets, etc. . . .

Another parent had this same concern as well and others began to murmur to each other as tension around the issue thickened. After a moment of thinking of a way to resolve the issue, Dr. Mims decided that since both of these parents had children in the kindergarten and they attended the lower grades campus, she would try to work with them. Yet, she was clearly not pleased finally telling them:

> I will let you all prepare lunches for the younger children but my decision is contingent upon the fact that your children will not be allowed to get a school lunch if they decide that on some days they may want what is being served at school . . . either they get the school's lunch or they don't.

Nevertheless, she was uncompromising about the issue with the new boarding school campus parents stating, "they won't bring food into the new school . . . that's just not happening." Finally, in closing the discussion, Dr. Mims encouraged other parents to trust her and "please stick with the mandatory school lunch program." She ended the discussion not letting the two parents off the hook so easily with a mini sermon/lecture:

> You know, when I was young, my parents put certain foods in front of me to eat and told me to "eat it, it's good for you!" And you know what, today they are calling those same foods health foods. Listen to me parents, you all had better be careful about letting your children at such an early age tell you what they will and will not eat. In a few years, they will be trying to tell you other things that they will and will not do. These will be unfortunate situations for you and your children in the long run—trust me, I've seen it happen on too many occasions.

Take control of your child's life right now! And begin to mold them into what you want them to be. When our children are babies, they are just like clay, and clay does not mold itself! I hope that you all are hearing me. I've seen it too many times. Soon the child will be bigger than you . . . then it'll be too late.

I could sense her sliding into the role of mother/elder/teacher as she responded to these young women and their concerns in reference to their children at such a young age deciding on whether or not they would eat the types of nutritious meals that they needed for nourishment, proper growth, and development. She ended her response to the parents by telling them, "start to talk to your children about what is good for them to eat and begin educating them on making the right choices and not always going for the foods that may taste really good but are very unhealthy for their minds and bodies."

This speech was grounded in the ways and days of the past when many African-American children were raised in quite strict ways in many instances as parents of the pre-Civil Rights years knew of the harshness of what could happen to a child who thought that they could do whatever they wanted in a usually hostile and white dominated society. Her narrative was quite powerful as I could see many of the parents in the audience nodding in approval of her comments directed specifically at the two mothers of the young students and indirectly at everyone. She was in many ways teaching the parents child rearing lessons from the African-American tradition.

Wisdom and School History from Mrs. Huff-Franklin

Mrs. Huff-Franklin's affiliations with MCPSC are far reaching. Obviously, a dedicated African-American woman whose vigor and dependability earned her lead-teacher status at the school, Mrs. Huff-Franklin was described in the 2000-2001 salutatorian graduation address as "the teacher of teachers." Reflections on the school during an interview with Mrs. Huff-Franklin helped to crack open a window into her reality and the way in which she perceived the school based on her experiences. She shared:

. . . I think it's kind of interesting . . . I was working in Cincinnati's public schools . . . as a long term substitute teacher so I had done a position that I had been at for about five or six months . . . and one of the teachers who . . . was actually related to one of my best friends had pulled me to the side and said "you know, you . . . you do so well with the students and there's this school that's starting. . . . Marva Collins, you heard of the Marva Collins in Chicago and they're trying to start up a school like that in Cincinnati" [she digresses] and this is before everybody was coming up with schools everywhere. . . . Marva Collins was the first in its time to be trying to start a new school . . . and my friend was telling me, "you know I think it's good to get in on the foundations of it" . . . and that's what first sparked my interest . . . when I looked in the newspaper then I saw the advertisement for it.

Particularly, the advertisement's qualifications really captured Mrs. Huff-Franklin's attention. The job announcement required a Liberal Arts background but did not solicit people who were looking for a job but looking to serve in a capacity similar to missionaries. Mrs. Huff-Franklin was inspired by the fact that Dr. Mims and others instrumental in the start of MCPSC were looking for teachers with missionary qualities and not simply someone who wanted a paycheck. Attracted to both the emphasis and zeal of an educational missionary, Mrs. Huff-Franklin's particularly long days (typically ten hours or more) at the school speak volumes.

Mrs. Huff-Franklin Speaks on Dedication and Commitment

. . . In our society, there's going to be a lot of people left behind . . . so, we want to keep our children here and keep them up at a high level. Even the worst acting at our school is going to be something . . . take Akil for instance, if he stays with us through eighth grade, and he has so many home problems or whatever, but you see, the biggest problem I have with him is saying, "put the book away," he likes to read. But we've been able to spark that interest in him. So, I don't mind having that discipline problem, because he likes to read . . . so if he hangs in there with us regardless of his bad background, he's going to be something . . . he's going to be somebody in society (she searches for words) . . . he won't go to prison. He'll be a productive citizen. . . .

. . . Now, up until this point, our school has been designed for students
of lower economic levels, those who might not be able to make it into
the more prestigious private schools in the city but have a lot of potential or those who sometimes came to us after being put out of the
public schools. For a long time, once they were put out of the public
schools and they didn't make it with us, they didn't have anywhere
else to go . . . because once they went back to public school it would
be the same cycle that they came to us for in the first place: kicked out,
suspended, expelled. They might be "smart as a whip" but they don't
sit like "Tommy" sits . . . see what I'm saying? Another example is
Sag, that's why I have him sitting way in the back . . . he'll be standing
up and nobody else would know it. See, he's just a little bit different,
but I can get a little more out of him . . . through patience, he's still
here and has not been expelled and has not been suspended. . . .

Mrs. Huff-Franklin: "A Vested Interest"

. . . you see, what they (outsiders of the MCPSC and the African-
American community) don't understand is that we have a vested interest . . . some teachers have the more typical, average public school
mentality towards our children (referring to African-American children) . . . referral, detention, suspension, and expulsion. But the difference here is, I feel, I have more of a vested interest in their future.
He or she and their family are going to live in my community, they
may end up marrying someone in my family. And, we can't afford to
see any of our people as being a lost because, we always have to look
for ways to help. . . .

We've been able to tap into different aspects (she was referring to
student performances and class poetry lessons) it has brought out the
leader in these children . . . those who others would have said were
discipline problems but they've evolved into leaders. Your discipline
problem kids are probably going to be your best leaders, because they're
not the type that likes to follow anyway. So, if you can get them to be
positive, then you know . . . they want to be the leader anyway. It's
just a matter of channeling and making them feel good enough about
themselves so that they could step down just a bit to let somebody else
lead until it's their turn.

Wisdom and School History from Mrs. Simmons

In an interview with Mrs. Simmons, I gained insights into how she became affiliated with MCPSC as well as some of her educational perspectives. Approximately ten years ago, Mrs. Simmons viewed an interview of Mrs. Marva N. Collins on the popular 60 Minutes television show. The interview covered various issues but there was a clear emphasis on educating Black children. Mrs. Simmons learned of many things about the Marva Collins philosophy that evening via the television program and was determined to one day learn more. Years later, and to her amazement, she learned of The Marva Collins Preparatory School located in her very own city of Cincinnati.

During the same period, Mrs. Simmons' sister was in attendance and in Dr. Mims' class at the local university where Dr. Mims served as a faculty member aside from her capacity as President/CEO of MCPSC. Mrs. Simmons shared with me:

> The one person that my sister talked about constantly was Dr. Mims . . . and I thought who is this lady because everyday . . . and I had gotten to the point where I would say "well what did Dr. Mims say today . . . what did Dr. Mims do today . . . what happened today with Dr. Mims in her class . . . Dr. Mims, Dr. Mims, Dr. Mims. . . .

> Finally, I thought I have to meet this lady. . . . So, I was going to [another city University] at the time and I decided well I think maybe I'll just transfer to the university where Dr. Mims teaches because my sister was taking this communications course and she was learning all these different things . . . and how to do things and say things . . . how to speak. So, I signed up for Dr. Mims' class and the very first night she spoke and gave us our syllabus I liked her . . . I thought wow, I see why my sister fell in love with Dr. Mims. . . .

Although Mrs. Simmons remembers this encounter quite vividly, these events had taken place fifteen to twenty years prior to our conversation. This long lasting effect and ability to win people's heart and commitment seems to be apparent in the President/CEO's interactions with Mrs. Simmons. In retrospect, Dr. Mims and Mrs. Simmons's first interactions were years before the inception of MCPSC, which opened in 1990.

While attending college, Mrs. Simmons simultaneously took early retirement from a major corporation in the city. And, after a year of "doing nothing" as she described it, "I began to get bored." This led to volunteer work in hospice services, insurance, and law offices, as well as tutoring and mentoring in the city's public schools.

A regular church going African-American woman who attends the oldest African Methodist Episcopal church in the city, Mrs. Simmons attributes a church sermon to influencing her to become a part of the MCPSC community. Her story is worth well worth documenting. She shared:

> One day I went to church and we had a really, really nice service about giving of yourself. . . . If you have something to give, give! You don't want to take it to your grave with you. So, I thought after I had heard this nice service at church you know what Dr. Mims at Marva Collins . . . I believe in that system . . . I think I'll send my resume to Dr. Mims. I sent it to her home and one night at about eleven o'clock I received a telephone call and Dr. Mims said . . . "I don't believe this . . . I am looking for somebody and you sent your resume to my home" . . . She went on, "meet me tomorrow at eleven and we'll talk . . . and today here I am.

After a long career in business, Mrs. Simmons's moral and ethical roots of "giving back" stemming from the black church and her previous interactions with the school's President/CEO influenced her decision and career path.

The Love and Elderly Wisdom of Mrs. Mayes

Insights from Mrs. Mayes, a God fearing woman always proved fruitful as she was able to provide even deeper insights into life at MCPSC as well as another perspective on her younger sister, Dr. Mims. During an interview, in a slow, soft-spoken voice filled with compassion, Mrs. Mayes shared several insights into her values, beliefs, and affiliations with the school.

> . . . oh . . . yes . . . I remember the school starting at the church . . . and I would go and help her clean the church . . . yes, I was helping her clean way back then . . . and my daughter had an apartment and we got this bed . . . a roll away bed and we brought that to the school for the children . . . so they'd have a place to lay down in the church. . . .

[Giving the praise to God] . . . we can go to heights where God want us to be . . . and that's who we should please everyday . . . our maker because he is about it all . . . he brought us this far . . . and I will never forget him, I cannot forget him . . . it's my personal thing . . . because it's God . . . it's all about God. . . . It's not predicated on Mrs. Mims . . . God uses all of us everyday . . . each one of the teachers . . . and all of us. . . .

Mrs. Mayes's presence in the dining area comforted students as her patience withstood major issues affecting the students' daily in their classes. A true optimist, she always saw light at the end of the tunnel, regardless of the situation.

Chapter 6

Surprise Guests at MCPSC

Surprise guests at MCPSC were a ritual in which the students really enjoyed. Dr. Mims worked diligently to bring meaningful experiences "into" their school. These visitors always seemed to add another layer of excellence to the MCPSC educational experience. Everyone seemed grateful. This chapter highlights some of these special moments that occurred during the 2000-2001 school year.

Dr. Mims's Surprise:
A Spontaneous Guest for the School
November 16, 2000

Today brought forth an interesting set of events as the President/CEO requested that I connect the new television and VCR in Mrs. Huff-Franklin's class. This event led to an interruption of the normal school day ritual. One student bubbling with excitement came to get me from down the hallway. He talked as he approached but in a failed whisper to me he said, "we need your help!" His sense of urgency sparked thoughts of a fight or some other sort of emergency in another part of the school.

It turned out that the President/CEO of the school had invited a local university professor to speak about his life to the entire school. What was to transpire in the next hour held the entire student population's attention as all seventy-five or so students sat comfortably (some on the floor) in the lead-teacher's room. This presentation went through the students lunch period, and most of them seemed not to be visibly con-

cerned with eating an hour later. In addition, Dr. Mims's spontaneous
supplements to the school's curriculum always overrode regular schoolhouse activity while also adding to the students' educational experiences.

Dr. Mims introduced the gentleman once the entire school was quietly seated in the room. The professor of African Haitian descent showed
the school a large picture reminiscent of those that hang on museum
walls for show. The picture was of a girl and he asked, "What do you
have in common with this little girl?" Students' hands went up sporadi-
cally, but before anyone was chosen someone yelled out, "she's black!"
This was the only answer given to the presenter's first question as some
began to snicker about the "black" remark. "What does this mean," he
went on but elicited no answers from students. After no other student
attempted to seek similarities he asserted, "yes this girl is black and she
is also from Haiti."

He went on to ask another question, "now, how did she get to Haiti?"
Some students raised their hands once more in the customary way as
others blurted out as though the school ritual of raise your hand before
speaking now did not apply in this case. "She flew from America?" . . .
"Train?" . . . "Boat?" The professor shook his head signaling "no" until
he heard "boat" come from the crowd, which caused him to focus on the
area from where the answer had come, "Yes, by boat!" He went on after
hearing a satisfactory answer, "How many of you have heard of slavery?" Many students raised their hands as he nodded in approval moving into lecture mode. Below is a paraphrase of the lecture as I attempted
to capture the essence of the presentation by sitting in the rear of the
crowded class:

> Around the 1600s our ancestors were brought over to this part of the
> world. . . . Christopher Columbus went to Haiti sent by his queen. . . .
> The people in Haiti at the time were not Africans like the girl you see
> on the picture, the people there were Indians like the Native American
> Indians that you all learn about. . . . Columbus forced Indians into
> slavery in order to take their gold and valuables. . . . Later the French
> took over and brought black people who they kidnapped from Af-
> rica. . . . A lot of slaves were dropped off in Virginia and other places
> such as Haiti. . . . You see this girl could be a descendent of the same
> place in Africa as your ancestors were and you are. . . . But while
> there was still slavery in the United States, Haiti had a revolution.
> "What is a revolution?"

A fourth grader, sitting in front with the 5/6th grade class responded, "when someone wants to take over the government and sometimes they fight others." I could see Dr. Mims, as she stood by the door, nodding and smiling in response to the boy's answer to the professor's question. This student was representing the school in a way that met her expectations. The professor continued his discussion:

> Haiti had a revolution in 1804 and America had one in 1865. Then later slavery was re-introduced in Haiti but on children. . . . (He refers to his picture) The little girl on this picture with the mud floor and broken wood for walls parents can't afford to take care of her so they made a deal with those people in Haiti with money to educate their children in return for the children's labor. The children are supposed to come back to help out their parents after their education and servitude is over, but what happens is the children never come back to take care of or help out their parents. They are kept as slaves. I was one of these children, my mother died when I was very young and my family sold me to this lady—I became a slave child. There are approximately 400,000 slave children today in Haiti. So, how did I get here? The people who owned me came to America when I was 14 years old. They then sent for me so that I could be their slave in America. They made me do all of the chores, clean, wash, everything for them but someone told them that they would get in trouble if they didn't put me in school. So, they didn't want to get in trouble and put me in a high school. I had a third grade education at this time.

He then passed around a leather strap that is used to beat the children before reading from a book that he had written on the experience. The students passed the leather strap around, as some of them winced at the thought of being hit with it. He went on:

> I had a favorite teacher who was a man that tutored and worked with me so that I could catch up with my peers. I was able to graduate and go to the Army with this teacher's assistance. From the Army, I went to a university in Florida, and then here to this city to attend one of the local universities. . . . At this point, I wrote a book.

The professor then wrote on the board that the title of his book means, "to stay with" because the children are not staying with their parents in Haiti. He brought along a video made by UNICEF to help him in getting rid of slavery in Haiti. He inserted the video into the newly installed classroom television and the entire school sat and watched.

Hip Hop Child Megastar
"Bow Wow" Visits MCPSC

Dr. Mims surprised everyone by calling a whole school assembly and escorting the *So So Def* recording label Rap Star, Bow Wow, into the chapel. During the week that followed, I was inundated with the latest emotional ravings of particularly the 7/8th grade girls in reference to Dr. Mims' surprise guest. The 7/8th grade girls maintained their emotional high longest of all. Actually, Bow Wow, at the time an eighth grader, was very close to their age, if not the same, and the fourth as well as 5/6th grade girls simply had to wait their turn. Below are compiled reactions and comments from students in reference to their surprise guest and Hip Hop rapper.

7/8th grade boys: not too emotional, seemed not all that impressed with Bow Wow and wondered what the girls in their class problem were. [Comments] "He alright." "Man those girls silly, actin' all crazy cause Bow Wow came here." "He aint nothin' but a boy just like us."

7/8th grade girls: still could not believe that Bow Wow was actually at their school and that they were able to touch him. A teacher informed me that most of the 7/8th grade girls were crying at the assembly when Bow Wow spoke to the school and on a Bow Wow emotional high for at least the next week. [Comments] "I want Bow Wow to be my man (meaning they wanted to court him)." "Bow Wow likes them Ghetto Girls, oh yeah."[1] "These boys at our school ain't nothin' but playa haters, they just trying to hate on Bow Wow cause we like him." "He is shorter than he look on T.V., but he still looks good." "I was about to pass out (faint)."

5/6th grade boys: rather envious but maintaining their "cool." Some mad nevertheless found laughter in the whole matter loosening their tensions for Bow Wow and his high jacking the MCPSC girls for a short moment. [Comments] "Man he was cool and everything." "I like them boots he was kicking' them junks was fresh." "Bow Wow stole our

---

1. He has a hit song entitled, "Ghetto Girls."

women . . . but it's all good cause he won't be here everyday." "Them girls was hatin' on us . . . they treated us like we were nothing . . . they didn't even see us." "I hate Bow Wow, I'll beat his butt." "I can understand those girls crying but David . . . he couldn't even sit in his seat right when he saw Bow Wow. He was so nervous and crying just like the girls . . . he fell out his seat when Bow Wow came in the room." "David said Bow Wow is my boyfriend," in which David categorically denied yelling, "no I didn't" (as they told me about David, I could not help but laugh at their imitations of him trembling uncontrollably and falling from his seat at the Bow Wow assembly.)

5/6th grade girls: mostly the same sentiments of the 7/8th graders with a bit lower intensity. [Comments] "My daddy is going to take us (two girls) to the Bow Wow concert in Dayton (about an hours drive)" "I couldn't help but cry, I couldn't believe it when Mrs. Mims brought Bow Wow in the chapel—I thought I was gonna faint." "Y'all was crying not me for no Bow Wow . . . get your facts straight" "Bow Wow fine (nice body)." "Them 7/8th grade girls was about to knock everybody down trying to touch him." "He gave that same little ole speech I heard him give on T.V. about make straight A's, keep faith in God, and do your work in school. I bet he don't have straight A's."

Fourth grade boys: typically in awe and adoration. Not as envious as the older classes of boys [Comments] "He was cool." "You saw what he had on, that junk was tight (his outfit was nice)!"

Fourth grade girls: typically in awe like the other girls. [Comments] "Bow Wow was fine." "He too big to be my boyfriend, but I like him anyway." "I see why all them girls be chasing him on them videos, it must be because he look so good."

These types of surprises in many ways deified Dr. Mims. She even had autographed posters for students with no "infractions" which meant no bus demerits or office visits for the year. One girl was flabbergasted when she did not receive a poster. After Dr. Mims had presented all posters for their class, the girl innocently remarked, "I didn't get one." Dr. Mims responded, "that is because you have infractions in your file" exiting the room.

MCPSC Alumnus Visits

On another occasion, I had the opportunity to witness MCPSC's 7/8th graders as they interacted with a former student who was now in the middle of her senior year of high school. "So what do y'all think about Jesse Jackson?" asked Janine probing the 7/8th graders' minds on Jesse Jackson's illegitimate child fiasco, which recently broke through the national media. Comments of, "that's just my baby daddy" came jokingly from several of the students as they imitated a popular recent Hip Hop song entitled *That's Just My Baby Daddy*.

This situation had Janine all excited at the gossipy nature of the topic while at the same time disappointed at such a poor representation of African-American leadership and lack of commitment to the integrity of his family. Before moving to another subject Janine remarked, "now we know why Rev. Jackson was so forgiving of President Clinton when he got in trouble with Monica Lewinsky, huh."

Janine was a seventh grader during my student teaching/internship days at MCPSC approximately five years ago, and popped by the new campus to pay a visit. Seizing on the teachable moment, Dr. Mims arranged for her to come and speak with the various classes in reference to her experiences after leaving MCPSC. I witnessed the 7/8th grade students interact with a MCPSC alumnus around several issues, but the core of her discussion focused on the "7 Hill Schools" of the city.[2]

> You all want to do as good as you can here at Marva Collins so that you can get accepted into one of the city 7 Hill Schools. And, believe me, none of you want to get caught up in those public schools. . . . Let me give you all an example of where I am coming from, I get to do all kinds of things at my school that you will never get to do in a public school. I just came from Europe for three weeks and when I leave here today, I'm going by a funeral home to arrange for a casket to be delivered to my school for a drunk driving presentation. Do you really think you're going to get those opportunities in the public schools?

Janine seemed to represent a level of hope for these students as many of them were in the second grade when she attended MCPSC's lower grades campus—when there was but one campus.

The students seemed to enjoy the dialogue with Janine, Janine as well. She shared with them how she was in the process of selecting a university to attend. She spoke of strong leanings toward a HBCU (His-

---

2. The city 7 Hill Schools were St. Xavier, St. Ursula, Cincinnati Hills, Cincinnati Country Day, Seven Hills, St. Ursuline, and Summit High School.

torically Black Colleges and Universities) as she candidly shared with the students that although her high school is one of the top in the city, she was one of few African-Americans at the school. "When I go off to college, I just want to be surrounded more by my own people," was her rationale as the students probed her on why a black college.

Finally, Janine admonished the class to do their best while at MCPSC, "because it's not going to be the same when you leave—trust me." In addition, before exiting Janine shared with the class that her family had traveled to Washington, D.C. for this year's Million Family March 2000 and that black people must always "stick" together. "No one is going to care as much about you all as Mrs. Huff-Franklin and these teachers around here. . . . So, respect them and do your best, because it will never be the same once you leave." Surely, MCPSC was a unique and meaningful place in the heart and mind of this alumnus—an experience she now seemed to appreciate and cherish. Furthermore, MCPSC students got a glimpse at what the future could hold, if they chose not to take their experience at MCPSC for granted.

Later in the year, Janine returned with another MCPSC's alumnus who had been home schooled after her departure and was now attending a local university. Dr. Mims gave both girls the task of connecting with their other classmates, so that she could meet with all of them in the future.

Chapter 7

Senior Week: It's So Hard to Say Goodbye

One of the most powerful rituals of senior week took place as the school staff and some parents organized a tribute to the school's eighth grade seniors in which they took a back seat as the younger students honored the MCPSC's graduates. On this particular day during the school's last week the lower grades campus staff and students took a trip to the higher grades boarding campus to participate in a ceremony to "send off the seniors." Also, invited to this event were the seniors' parents. Thus, on this day, the chapel was filled with students from both campuses as the seniors sat in a semicircle taking in the shower of praise heaped on them by their fellow schoolmates.

Tribute to Seniors Day seemed to symbolically represent the seniors "last walk in the sun" during a regular school day. Informed to "dress up" and shed the school's uniform, the six girls all wore very elegant, sleeveless, summer dresses with classy ladies pumps to match. The boys sported a business casual look as they wore slacks and collared button up shirts. This was an opportunity to separate themselves from the other students at the school as well as give them something in which to look forward. The eight students graced the stage on this day as if they were mature young adults. As a sign of this new felt maturity, each of the girls sat with their legs crossed on this day. They all represented themselves in a very regal manner.

On this day, the seniors simply sat as the kindergarten thru third grade students came up to the stage and gave farewell speeches that they had obviously been preparing for with their teachers at their respective

campus. The students came up in small groups resembling a line of duck-
lings and recited such poems as "Be Strong" or "A Great Somebody"
from the MCPSC classics list of poetry. In addition, other students from
the lower grades campus individually presented small gifts and cards that
they had made in school to the seniors as going away memoirs. Finally,
one small boy who looked to be in the first or second grade came to the
front of the platform in which the seniors sat and honored them by sing-
ing a touching solo. I was not familiar with this song, but the small boy
seemed to sing it in a touching, meaningful way—from the heart. He was
not shy or bashful and before he had completed the song, three of the
senior girls were crying. And, as I peered into the audience, I noticed
some to the parents crying as well. Dr. Mims seeming to have prepared
for the effects of this ritual, sat to the right of the stage equipped with a
box of Kleenex passing them out and wiping her eyes occasionally.

The fifth, sixth and seventh graders from the higher grades campus
did not perform tributes. Yet, most of these students sat with their eyes
glued to the front as the seniors stood and delivered their "last words" to
the school following the young boy's solo.

After two of the eighth grade seniors had given their remarks, I
knew that preparing their "last words" had been one of Dr. Mims special
end of the year assignments for the seniors. Each of the students' "last
words" were structured in a very similar fashion. First, there was thanks
and honor given to their respective families followed by acknowledgment of the teachers who had impacted their lives. They all ended their
speeches with promises to give back to MCPSC after achieving their
career goals of becoming lawyers, pediatricians, professional actresses,
engineers, and architects. Each of the student's speeches had caveats,
which deviated from the basic group structure allowing for a more per-
sonalized story. Latasha shared her story of being born a miracle child
weighing only a little over one pound but surviving against the odds.
Alonzo, spoke of all the values he had learned from his aunt, Mrs. Huff-
Franklin as he personally addressed her using her first name, which was
touching and appropriate for this particular occasion. Leroy touched the
crowd as he gave thanks to his mother sitting in the audience for putting
up with him as a widowed mother after his father's death several years
ago. Diane, thanked the teachers for putting up with her "attitude" over
the years telling the staff, "I know that I haven't been the best student,
but I promise that I won't let you all down. . . . I am going to be somebody and make you all proud." Berniece and Donyetta thanked Dr. Mims

for taking them all over the country speaking to people and raising money for the school. Donyetta also told her, "Dr. Mims, you have even taken us almost around the world when you took us to South Africa."

By the time each student completed their speeches, they, their parents, and many students and staff were in tears. Dr. Mims saw fit to go and stand with her arms around Leroy and Latasha as they cried blurring the words of their speeches. With the exception of Latasha who had been at the school for three years at that time, most of these students had been a student at MCPSC since at least the third grade. Furthermore, Leroy was one of the school's first students having been a student in the first school in the church basement, the school after it moved to the lower grades campus, and finally attending the higher grades boarding school. He was MCPSC's longest standing student and a shining example of the institution's capability, as Dr. Mims would often say, "only if we had them from the cradle." Leroy had been accepted and was headed to one of the more prestigious and reputable private high schools in the city the following year—one of the "7 Hill Schools of Cincinnati".

Afterwards, Dr. Mims shared with me her rationale for such an event highlighting where and how she came up with such a ritual practice. She explained,

> Well, I lie in my bed at night and think all of these things through. Then, when I get up in the mornings I have my visions of exactly what it is that I want to do . . . the next step is only putting my visions into action . . . that's where this Senior Tribute Day idea came from. . . .

> . . . You see, I want it to be an occasion where the teachers all step back and let the students talk to and honor each other. I feel as if the teacher should have said what they needed to say to them by then. So, now it's their schoolmates turn. I wanted to send the seniors off with something special and I wanted them to see what they are leaving behind. That way they will understand that for this institution to go on, they will have to come back, give back, and help. I also wanted to give those seniors a chance to stand up and say what's on their minds . . . to tell us how they feel and to give thanks to all who have helped them get to where they are. You know this is very important . . . that they are given the forum to share their last words. Through this process of sharing and being showered with love and gifts from their peers, an emotional bond is created between them and this school that they will carry with them for the rest of their lives. . . .

A Picturesque Senior Moment

On another occasion, I noticed the eighth grade students sitting quietly alone in the dining area. In the hallway leading to the dining area were eight neatly hung white sheets of computer papers with digitized pictures of each senior standing individually in front of the school's sign in the school yard. Above each senior's picture was their name all typed bold and capital letters and beneath each picture was the school in which the students would be attending the following year. Each of these students were going to prestigious private as well as public schools of the city—a fact that made the staff quite proud. As I entered the dimly lit room, they all sat reclining in their chairs as if I had interrupted a good meditation session. Donyetta, Alonzo, Berniece, Diane, Latasha, Leroy, Brianna, and Beverly all seemed much more mature as they all sat together—they were the eighth grade seniors with privileges.

I knew that the students had been working on projects created and administered by Dr. Mims so I asked, "so what's this project all about that you all are doing that gets you all out of class?" Berniece, the school's eventual Valedictorian spoke first "this project that we are working on now is on racial profiling for Dr. Mims." Latasha corrected her, "actually it's for us, Dr. Mims just gave it to us." Then, Beverly chimed in, "See, it's this project that we have to put our heads together and finish it." Berniece clarified their project even more, "we have to put our heads together and figure out a problem or something that has been a problem in society and we all have to propose the best possible solution using teamwork." Finally, Alonzo chimed in with another interesting perspective on the issue saying, "see, that's what we have to do and then when we finish, she can go and take it to show to people and say, see look how good my little kiddies did . . . give us some money!" The girls refuted his comments saying, "no, it's not like that" forcing him to rephrase his point. He tried again, "nah, it's not exactly like that, she doesn't say give me some money right then, but she always taking and showing off our work to all different types of people—and they do give us money sometimes."

Before leaving, I asked Alonzo had he ever heard of human capital. This question drew a table full of blank stares. Therefore, I went into a mini explanation:

You all are in many ways human capital for this school. Dr. Mims shows you all off . . . show how bright you all are and at the same time people like to hear that and they give certain things to keep the school going. So, the school continues for those who will come after you. Do you think that's fair?

Shrugging his shoulders, Alonzo replied, "that's fair, why not?"

The issue of racial profiling was surely one of the burning societal problems that indicated the students, all African-American, awareness of at least one factor that has direct and indirect effects on their immediate lives. I later learned that Dr. Mims was rather impressed with the students' final proposed solution which entailed putting in place ways for the police to be policed themselves. These assignments were precious and a last battery of tests prescribed by Dr. Mims as if the seniors were being initiated into the inner sanctums of a MCPSC Alumni Society.

During an interview, Dr. Mims shared insights into why she chose to implement such end of the year rituals.

First of all, I know each child by that time and I know what each child needs. Take for example, a Diane . . . an attitudinal problem. So, my subject may be, "you're very very bright. You're very, very beautiful. You have all of these things" and I want them to know that I know all of these things about them. It's as if someone is evaluating you. "But, there's one weakness . . . that you have to work on, and that's your attitude." So, I will get into a lecture on attitude and I will make it so simple by using parables and asking them questions. It's very philosophical what I'm doing . . . but I will talk about attitude.

If it's a Sharon, I would say, "respect" . . . because Sharon thinks that everything" [she digresses] I'm talking about them because I know each individual . . . and I know what their weaknesses are. So, if it's a Sharon . . . Sharon's weakness is that I (refereeing to Sharon) thinks that everything should be fair. Smart, but . . . am I not hitting them on the head? [I smile nodding in agreement as I, too, know these students very well] Everything should be fair. Well, my philosophical conversation with Sharon would center around fairness and what is fairness— life is not fair. You know what I mean. Just conversation, just communication, giving them an opportunity one on one to express themselves without having to feel that they are being put down in front of their peers. You can't do that in the classroom, you have to do that one on one . . . And then you have to do it in very small groups. . . .

We don't have a counselor and it's like counseling to me, you see. I do it all yearlong when it's needed but I do it at the end of the year when I know they are leaving me. I don't want to leave anything unsaid. So, I want their attention!

In reference to the garden that the seniors had to create in the south/east corner of the school, the President/CEO shared,

They always must do something to give back, something that is permanent . . . something that one-day they can come back, look, and say, "this is what we left behind". And it's something that they left behind that's concrete and they are excited about that. . . .

The children planted a tree down at the other school, some of them graduated and they went out there and they saw it after their graduation. It's important to the kids to be able to leave something, to give something. And, I'm also trying to plant the seed that giving is always better than receiving. And, It's just as when I received that honorary doctorate degree—I made a big deal of it with them. And, I remember one of the things that I definitely said was, "well you know all of the other degrees that you get, you are gaining something . . . you get a degree and that degree is measured by how much you have gained . . . how much knowledge you've gotten from the books and all of that is for yourself. You walk across the stage and they give you this doctorate degree. But, this honorary doctorate degree is similar to that but it's measured only by how much you give. So, it's different in that sense." And they understood my point.

Dr. Mims went on to tell me of how the students could relate to her message and how important it is that she "leave no stone unturned" before sending them away. In her final assessment she shared, "if they stay with us long enough, we will pin so many wings on them, they will have no choice but to fly."

References

Asante, M. (1998). *The Afrocentric idea*. Philadelphia, PA: Temple University Press.

Dabney, W. P. (1926). *Cincinnati's colored citizens* (Vol. 8). Cincinnati, OH: The Dabney Publishing Company.

Delagdo, R., & Stefancic, J. (1997). *Critical white studies: Looking behind the mirror*. Philadelphia, PA: Temple University Press.

Gaston, A., Kelley, S., Knight Abowitz, K., Rousmaniere, K., & Solomon, W. (1999). *Collaboration within and without: The case study of Taft High School*. Cincinnati, OH: Ohio Department of Education.

Glickman, C. (1993). *Renewing America's Schools: A guide for school-based action*. San Fransisco, CA: Jossey-Bass.

Harland, R. (1987). *Superstructuralism: The philosophy of structuralism and post-structuralism*. London, New York: Methuen.

Macke, S. M. (1999). *The struggles of Cincinnati's black community for educational opportunity in the 19th century. Paper presented at the 1999 annual meeting of the American Educational Studies Association in Detroit, MI*. Unpublished manuscript, Terre Haute, IN.

McIntosh, P. (1989). White privilege: Unpacking the invisible knapsack. *Peace and Freedom*, 10-12

Robinson, R. (2000). *The debt: What America owes to Blacks*. New York: Dutton.

Woodson, C. G. (1916). Negroes of Cincinnati prior to Civil War. In W. P. Dabney (Ed.), *Cincinnati's Colored Citizens* (Vol. 1, pp. 25-43). Cincinnati, OH: The Dabney Publishing Company.

Woodson, C. G. (1993). *The mis-education of the negro*. Trenton, N.J.: Africa World Press.

About the Author

Originally from Belle Glade Florida, Dr. P. Collins completed undergraduate and masters level studies at both The University of Central Florida and Florida A&M University. In addition to graduating with high academic honors, he also played baseball on the collegiate level and was selected as an Academic All-American in his final season at Florida A&M University.

Dr. Collins served several years as a professional educator in Florida's public schools before moving on to complete doctoral studies in Educational Leadership at Miami University of Ohio. Additionally, he has worked in various roles with the Marva Collins Preparatory School of Cincinnati, OH, an independent educational institution. He has worked with American military dependents during summers on U.S. military bases in Panama City Florida, Yukusoka Japan, and Oahu Hawaii.

His pedagogical and research interests are in the areas of critical transformative educational leadership, Afrocentric discourse, and the intersections of education and social justice.

Currently, Dr. Collins is an Assistant Professor in the Division of Education at Baldwin-Wallace College. He teaches courses in Educational Foundations as well as Early Childhood Education. In addition, Dr. Collins plans to teach several other courses in his field in the near future.